1

# THE BLINKING EYE:

## RALPH WALDO ELLISON

and his American, French, German and
Italian Critics, 1952-1971

Bibliographic Essays and a Checklist

by

## JACQUELINE COVO

The Scarecrow Author Bibliographies, No. 18

## The Scarecrow Press, Inc.
## Metuchen, N.J. 1974

This book contains in much altered updated form portions of material reprinted by permission of CLA Journal as follows:

Sections of the U.S. essays and checklist, 1952-1964, CLA Journal, 15 (December, 1971), 171-196.

A truncated summary of the French essays and checklist, CLA Journal, 16 (June, 1973), 519-526.

Library of Congress Cataloging in Publication Data

Covo, Jacqueline.
   The blinking eye.

   (The Scarecrow author bibliographies, no. 18)
   1. Ellison, Ralph.  2. Ellison, Ralph—Bibliography.  I.  Title.
PS3555.L625Z63      016.818'5'409      74-13042
ISBN 0-8108-0736-X

To the memory of my grandparents,
Flor and Israel Nissim,
who perished in the Holocaust

The man bent over his guitar,
A shearsman of sorts.   The day was green.

They said, "You have a blue guitar,
You do not play things as they are."

The man replied, "Things as they are
Are changed upon the blue guitar."

And they said then, "But play, you must,
A tune beyond us, yet ourselves,

A tune upon the blue guitar
Of things exactly as they are."

(Wallace Stevens)*

# PREFACE

This book was undertaken with a dual aim: to provide a broad range of multinational reference materials for the study of Ralph Ellison, and to allow some suggestive cross-cultural comparison of the responses elicited by his work, from 1952, the year of Invisible Man's publication, through 1971. Under the former heading, the checklist brings together a reasonably comprehensive listing of criticism which in the case of the United States had not yet been systematically compiled, and in the case of the three European countries surveyed was largely unavailable in any form. With respect to the second aim, it is hoped that the essays will provide an analysis of each country's reaction and will facilitate comparisons between them.

A variety of unforeseen problems slowed down research almost beyond reason: for the American criticism, the abundance of material and the endless number of very selective indices available, posed one kind of difficulty. Just the opposite was true with respect to Europe; here the almost total lack of bibliographic tools, combined with the very selective U. S. library holdings of foreign journals and newspapers, and the inevitable time lag in publication of such materials stimulate the imagination to utopian fancies-- of computerized research services, a man on call in every major European library, travel funds, and the lifespan of the patriarchs.

With minimal exceptions, each item in the checklists has been seen and read. Although every effort has been made to ensure completeness of the criticism, the search of anthologies, histories, and reference works has, of necessity, not been exhaustive, though I trust it is representative. Unpublished dissertations have as far as possible been included in the checklists, but not in the discussion. Because of the difficulties outlined above, no systematic search of translations was made with respect to Ellison's short fiction and essays.

The original aim of including essays and a checklist
of British criticism was unfortunately rendered impossible,
as this would have unduly delayed publication and dated the
1971 cutoff. For the convenience of the interested reader,
a very selective checklist of such British and Commonwealth
secondary material as was available to me will be found
without accompanying discussion at the end of the book.

Unless otherwise stated, all translations of foreign
materials quoted in the essays are mine. For convenience,
all publication titles have been abbreviated in the essays,
following the conventional MLA abbreviations wherever possible.

The most joyful part of this undertaking is to thank
all those whose contributions made it possible, while ab-
solving them of all responsibility for its shortcomings. I
conceived and began the work at the University of Chicago,
where thanks to a postdoctoral Black Studies Fellowship
from the Danforth Foundation, I was privileged to spend
the academic year 1970-1971, enriched by contact with
Professor John Hope Franklin and his colleagues. Professor George D. Kent of the University of Chicago encouraged
the project, was generous with his interest and advice, and
read the initial portion of the manuscript. Very special
thanks are due to Mrs. Fanny Ellison, who in the final
and crucial stages of the work answered queries and ran-
sacked her files for missing material with unparalleled
patience and courtesy. I am also grateful to Mr. Warren
Bower of the School of Continuing Education, New York
University, Mr. Studs Terkel of WFMT Radio, Chicago,
and Mr. R. Stewart Lillard of the South Carolina State Library at Columbia, S. C., for information on tapes and other
unpublished materials. Mr. Harry Wohlmuth of Chicago
skillfully translated much of the Italian criticism. Miss
Aimé Kangro, reference librarian, and Miss Helen Smith,
interlibrary loans librarian, both of the University of Chicago, as well as Sister Mary Agnes Powers, C.S.J., interlibrary loans librarian at Regis College, Weston, Massachusetts, all contributed their expertise with dispatch and
good cheer. I am also indebted to the following: Mr.
Ernest Kaiser of the Schomburg Library in New York, Miss
Christiane Laude of the Benjamin Franklin Documentation
Center in Paris, France, Mr. Robert D. Armstrong, Special Collections Librarian, the University of Nevada in
Reno, Professor Elizabeth C. Phillips, Memphis State University, and Mr. Hartmut K. Selke, Kiel University, West
Germany; also to the libraries at the University of Chicago,

the Center for Research Libraries in Chicago, the Widener
Library and the New England Deposit Library in Cambridge,
Massachusetts.  Mr. Ellison's foreign publishers, Editions
Bernard Grasset, Paris, Fischer Verlag, Frankfurt, Victor
Gollancz, Ltd. , London, Martin, Secker & Warburg, Ltd. ,
London, and Giulio Einaudi S. P. A. , Torino, were most
cooperative.  Mrs. Genevieve B. Childs typed the manuscript
with consummate skill and patience; my husband, Abe, faith-
fully picked up the debris in the wake of each crisis.   To
all these, and to any whom I may inadvertently have omitted,
I wish to express my very warmest appreciation and gratitude.


                              Jacqueline Covo,
                              Regis College,
                              Weston, Massachusetts

# TABLE OF ABBREVIATIONS

| | |
|---|---|
| AForum | African Forum: A Quarterly Journal of Contemporary Affairs |
| AJSoc | American Journal of Sociology |
| Approdo | L'Approdo Letterario |
| AR | Antioch Review |
| ArQ | Arizona Quarterly |
| ASch | American Scholar |
| BB | Bücherei und Bildung |
| BFLS | Bulletin de la Faculté des Lettres de Strasbourg |
| BK | Die Bücherkommentare |
| BlackAR | Black Academy Review |
| BlackW | Black World (formerly Negro Digest) |
| Book Week | New York Herald Tribune Book Week |
| BZ | Badische Zeitung |
| CalEJ | California English Journal |
| CCa | La Civiltà Cattolica |
| CJF | Chicago Jewish Forum |
| CLAJ | College Language Association Journal |
| CN | Cinema Nuovo |
| ColQ | Colorado Quarterly |
| ConL | Contemporary Literature (Supersedes WSCL) |
| CR | Chicago Review |
| CW | Christ und Welt |
| DAW | Sitzungsberichte der Deutschen Akademie der Wissenshaften zu Berlin |

| | |
|---|---|
| DStZ | Deutsche Studentenzeitung |
| DZ | Deutsche Zeitung und Wirtschaftszeitung |
| EJ | English Journal |
| ER | English Record |
| Esp | L'Espresso |
| FAZ | Frankfurter Allgemeine Zeitung |
| FiL | La Fiera Letteraria |
| FL | Figaro Littéraire |
| FNP | Frankfurter Neue Presse |
| FR | Frankfurter Rundschau |
| FV | Fränkischer Volksfreund |
| GdE | Gazzetta dell'Emilia |
| GdP | Gazzetta di Parma |
| Ge | Gegenwart |
| GM | La Gazzetta del Mezzogiorno |
| HA | Hamburger Anzeiger |
| HP | Hannoversche Presse |
| HudR | Hudson Review |
| I&D | Informations et Documents |
| ICS | L'Italia che scrive |
| IKZ | Illustrierte Kronen - Zeitung |
| IR | Iowa Review |
| JAF | Journal of American Folklore |
| JAmS | Journal of American Studies |
| JAS | Jahrbuch für Amerikastudien |
| JEGP | Journal of English and Germanic Philology |
| JPC | Journal of Popular Culture |
| KL | Kunst und Literatur |
| KR | Kenyon Review |
| LanM | Les Langues Modernes |
| LetF | Lettres Françaises |
| LetN | Les Lettres Nouvelles |

| | |
|---|---|
| LJ | Library Journal |
| MASJ | Midcontinent American Studies Journal |
| MedR | Mediterranean Review |
| MFS | Modern Fiction Studies |
| MM | Münchner Merkur |
| Mondo | Il Mondo |
| MR | Massachusetts Review |
| NA | Nuova Antologia |
| NALF | Negro American Literature Forum |
| NConL | Notes on Contemporary Literature |
| ND | Negro Digest |
| NR | New Republic |
| NS | Die Neueren Sprachen |
| NSM | Neusprachliche Mitteilungen |
| NV | Neue Volksbildung |
| NYHT | New York Herald Tribune |
| NYT | New York Times |
| NZZ | Neue Zürcher Zeitung |
| PA | Présence Africaine |
| PP | Paris Presse |
| PR | Partisan Review |
| PS | Paese-Sera |
| PubW | Publishers' Weekly |
| RGB | Revue Générale Belge |
| RLV | Revue des Langues Vivantes |
| SA | Studi Americani |
| SBL | Studies in Black Literature |
| SBV | Sonnenberg Briefe zur Völkerverständigung |
| SdZ | Süddeutsche Zeitung |
| SewR | Sewanee Review |
| SF | Sinn und Form |
| SHR | Southern Humanities Review |

| | |
|---|---|
| SN | Studies in the Novel |
| Sp | Lo Spettatore Italiano |
| SQ | Sociological Quarterly |
| SR | Saturday Review |
| StB | Sonntagsblatt |
| StZ | Stuttgarter Zeitung |
| SWR | Southwest Review |
| TCL | Twentieth Century Literature |
| TriQ | Tri-Quarterly |
| TS | Der Tagesspiegel |
| TSLL | Texas Studies in Literature and Language |
| UDQ | University of Denver Quarterly |
| WB | Die Welt der Bücher (Literarische Beihefte zur Herder-Korrespondenz) |
| WHR | Western Humanities Review |
| WSCL | Wisconsin Studies in Contemporary Literature |
| WWR | Walt Whitman Review |
| WZ | Wiener Zeitung |
| XUS | Xavier University Studies |
| YR | Yale Review |
| ZAA | Zeitschrift für Anglistik und Amerikanistik (East Berlin) |

# TABLE OF CONTENTS

xiv

UNITED STATES - ESSAYS

# INTRODUCTION

As everyone knows, many trees have fallen in the service of American Ellison scholarship, whose bulk, especially in the past six years, threatens to run the reader underground. The criticism falls into two distinct categories, reflecting historical, cultural and aesthetic changes: the first period, 1952-1964, is bounded by the publication of Invisible Man and Shadow and Act at either end; the second, 1965-1971 reflects dramatically the changes consequent upon the advent of the Black Power and Black nationalistic movements. Ellison's significance and major status are recognized from the first, but the quality of the attention he elicits varies with the times. Critical assessments in the early period are predominantly white, for the most part "objective" and analytical but (with honorable exceptions) share a tendency once described by Saunders Redding as "the minimizing of Negro writing as projections of a significant aspect of American reality and a distinctive American experience" ("Problems of the Negro Writer," MR, 6, Autumn-Winter, 1964-1965). In different ways, both white and black critics may be faulted on this score. The later period is marked by the far greater impact of black scholarship; on the one hand criticism both white and black broadens perceptibly, while on the other, scholarship itself is inevitably infected by the convulsions and rhetorical extravagances of the times.

It is also worth noting that from its first publication Invisible Man--which, among all Ellison's writings is still the center of attention--led its public life in an anomalous atmosphere of reader preconceptions and mixed motives. Except for its source, the insistence that book and author should express reality on the readers' terms rather than on their own has remained unchanged: in the early period the pressure of subtle white racial attitudes predominates, while in the later period the source of pressure shifts vocally to black readers and opinion makers. The responsibility of book and author as defined (or assumed) by others has

3

ranged from the demand that they display mandatory racial
scars to the requirement that they conform to arbitrary literary standards for "Negro" literature, involving everything
from the duty of tracing the Negro's assimilation to that of
vaunting his blessed separateness.

These factors, added to Invisible Man's own inexhaus-
tible richness, account for the great range of critical approaches, as well as for the extremes of opinion it has
elicited.  It has thrived under the sustained application of
white New Criticism methods, proved recalcitrant to the
scrutiny of biracial Marxist critics, and is now beginning
a slow ascent among proponents of the new "black aesthetic."
Its protagonist interpreted as everything from Odysseus to
clown engaged in a variety of quests ranging from epic to
demonic, the book has been acclaimed as "a triumph of art
and the moral imagination," and rejected as a moral failure:
the eye of the beholder has perceived Ellison in equally extreme guises as Uncle Tom, "Brown-skinned aristocrat,"
zoot-suiter, of central significance as well as totally irrelevant.  And while criticism these days seems much more
sharply divided along color lines, another major and encouraging trend is the much increased white sensitivity to
the black presence and cultural experience, which draws
some biracial criticism closer into a common perspective.
The observer can thus find reason to deplore a critical rut
as well as to look forward to a new greening of the scholarly
imagination.

The available material has been subdivided for discussion purposes, although this entails unavoidable overlapping and some duplication.  The headings in the Bibliography correspond to those in the essays.

# I. BIOGRAPHICAL INFORMATION

## 1952-1964

Although Ralph Ellison has been writing and publishing since 1937, he was almost unknown until the publication of his widely acclaimed novel, Invisible Man, in 1952. (Hereafter, I.M.) Not even Negro reference sources such as Who's Who in Colored America (7th ed., 1950), or Negro Yearbook (1952), include entries about him. Since 1952, biographical material has become available, beginning with Harvey Breit's rather superficial "portrait" of Ellison in a May 4, 1952, NYT interview. One of the earliest and most useful reference sources is the Biography Index with yearly entries beginning in its second volume (1953). In 1954 the fifth edition of World Biography and of Who's Who in America follow suit. The lengthiest and most informative listing is contained in Contemporary Authors, Vols. 11-12 (1962). Particularly useful features are detailed dates and a brief listing of books and magazines containing Ellison's work, as well as of major critical reviews. Since 1952 one may also count on the NYT and the Afro-American press to chronicle major events in Ellison's career, such as his receiving the Russwurm Award and the National Book Award in 1953, and his election to the National Institute of Arts and Letters in 1964. Though complementary, most of these sources are, inevitably, still less than complete.

A fruitful introduction to Ellison's intellectual background (as opposed to strictly factual material), is available in the interviews he granted. There are five interviews in 1952-1964; those in Paris Review (1955), Phoenix and December (both in 1961), provide valuable but not easily accessible insights into the author's formative childhood experiences and present attitudes. The leitmotif of cultural pluralism which is later to become such a controversial issue is already quite fully developed here. By 1964, the close of this first period under consideration, many of these

5

major interviews are made available by being collected in
Ellison's second book, <u>Shadow and Act.</u>

1965-1971

This period is only half the length of the preceding
twelve-year span, but is crucial in terms of developments
in Ellison's reputation.   In 1965, I.M. was polled the most
important novel since World War II (see p. 23), thus giving
further impetus to the growing interest in its author.   Also
in this period, Ellison's rise to eminence within the ranks
of white America's cultural elite (attested by a variety of
honors and high positions in respected cultural institutions),
contrasts sharply with the growing rift between him and one
portion of his black readership, over the question of political
ideology in art.

One consequence of these developments is an extraordinary focus on Ellison's personality and on biographical
matters normally separate from aesthetic considerations.
Already prefigured in the Irving Howe-Ralph Ellison debate
in the pages of <u>Dissent</u> (Autumn, 1963) and the <u>New Leader</u>
(February, 1964), the polemics regarding Ellison's position
on art, negritude and the relationship between the two, now
swell alarmingly in bulk and stridency, blocking the reader's
direct encounter with Ellison's work.   Whereas in the earlier
period serious enquiry into the "authenticity" of Ellison's
blackness might have seemed irrelevant to the understanding
of his book, in 1965-1971 it appears at times as though the
expression of views on that question has superseded all
other critical considerations.   Thus, the student is faced at
this time with an uncommonly large amount of biographical
material, much of it slanted by friend and critic alike, and
almost forcing the reader into taking a hasty position himself, in order to cope with his reading.   Moreover, he is
faced with drought amidst plenty, for information of a more
conventional kind, such as the extent of Ellison's European
travels and contacts is simply not available, though such
knowledge would be of undoubted value to the study of this
writer.

In examining the more conventional biographical
reference entries available on Ellison, one finds that they
are still likely to be more abundant in white rather than in
black sources.   The "Biographical Dictionary" of the <u>Negro</u>

Handbook (1966) for example, omits Ellison entirely, and in-
clusions of him, as in the International Library of Negro
Life and History (1968) or the Negro Almanac (1967), seem
sketchy. By 1971, a rather more detailed entry may be
found in E. Toppin's A Biographical History of Blacks in
America Since 1528. In contrast, a lengthy and informative
listing appears much earlier in Contemporary Authors, a
white source (Vols. 11-12, 1962). Though the editors of
Current Biography take no notice of Ellison until 1968, their
entry is equally helpful. Partly based on material from
Contemporary Authors, it, however, quotes more excerpts
from reviews, and also uses material from an interview
(John Corry, NYT, November 20, 1966) to provide the chatty
sort of personal portrait that might appeal to a wider public.
Somewhat incomplete, though quite helpful, is the "Chron-
ology of Important Dates" supplied by John M. Reilly in his
Twentieth Century Interpretations of "Invisible Man" (1970),
pp. 113-115. Here the tabulation chronicles Ellison's development in context with major contemporaneous cultural
and Civil Rights events in the United States.

Further interview material is also available in this
period, giving rise to Ernest Kaiser's caustic observation
that "Ellison has been interviewed and had his personal life
described more than many Hollywood and TV celebrities...."
(BlackW, December, 1970). Repeatedly, and at increasing
length, these interviews cover the same ground, stressing
Ellison's intellectual reserve and refined tastes--see notably
Richard Kostelantez' 1969 "Novelist as Brown-Skinned Aristocrat"--exploring his ideas and pluralistic cultural perspective, and evaluating the same according to the interviewer's
own preconceptions. To date, Ellison's Shadow and Act
(1964) still offers the best available insight into his mind
and art.

Notwithstanding the limelight in which the controversy
has placed him, Ellison still manages to surround himself
with an aura of privacy and aloofness which, together with
some of his expressed opinions, has provoked many black
intellectuals to accuse him of hostility. The time is de-
cidedly not ripe for the undertaking of a critical biography
to assess the range of Ellison's unique contribution to
America.

## II.  BIBLIOGRAPHIES

### 1952-1964

Though much was already being written on Ellison in this period, hardly any bibliographical work was being done.  Anyone attempting to compile his own list would find reference works either ignoring Ellison altogether (as in America in Fiction:  an Annotated List of Novels that Interpret Aspects of Life in the United States, Otis W. Coan and Richard G. Lillard, eds., 4th ed., 1956), or in the case of primary bibliographies, making no attempt to indicate that Ellison had ever written anything besides Invisible Man (e.g., Maxwell Whiteman, A Century of Fiction by American Negroes 1853-1952, Philadelphia, 1955).  For secondary materials information is only slightly more available and is equally scattered.  Ellison is totally excluded from Jacob Blanck's Bibliography of American Literature (1959); nor does he have an individual listing in the bibliography volume of Spiller's Literary History of the United States, 3rd ed. (1963).  The listings in Gerstenberger and Hendrick's The American Novel (1961) and D. Nyren's A Library of Literary Criticism, 3rd ed. (1964) are very scanty (four and six items respectively with duplications), and neither work includes entries beyond 1954.

### 1965-1971

This five-year period sees development of much more systematic bibliographies, especially toward the end of the 1960's.  To date, more attention has quite properly been focused on the area of primary work, beginning in 1968 with R. Stewart Lillard's most valuable bibliography of Ellison's fiction and essays for the period 1939-1967. This list, often indicating the reprint location as well as the original publication source, is an extremely valuable tool for the Ellison student, especially with respect to the earlier, generally neglected writings.  A 1969 "Addenda to

'A Ralph Waldo Ellison Bibliography' 1914-1968" by Carol
Polsgrove furnishes some additional items.   Apparently,
however, Lillard's and Polsgrove's work is not too widely
known, and does not seem to have been used by other re-
searchers.

James A. Emanuel and Theodore L. Gross, the
editors of Dark Symphony (1968), provide a handy list of
Ellison's short stories, but omit three stories included in
Lillard ("Birthmark, " 1940, "The Roof, the Steeple, and the
People, " 1960, "Juneteenth, " 1965).   In addition, the date
for "And Hickman Arrives, " is erroneously given as 1956,
rather than 1960.   Frank E. Moorer's and Lugene Baily's
"A Selected Check List ... " in BlackW (December, 1970)
does not appear to have had reference to Lillard's work in
its preparation; it rather seems to have been based partly
upon the Dark Symphony list, for it repeats the latter's
omissions, as well as the erroneous date for "and Hickman
... "   It does, however, add one short story not noted by
Lillard:   "It Always Breaks Out, " PR (Spring, 1963), 13-
38, and it updates the fiction list to 1970.   Supplementing
these lists and simultaneously replacing the usual chronological organization of writings by a genre classification (fiction, book reviews, literary and social essays, art and
music criticism), is Bernard Benoit's and Michel Fabre's
1971 "A Bibliography of Ralph Ellison's Published Writings, "
covering the period 1937 to June, 1971.

Ellison's writings themselves are being collected in
the University of Nevada's Modern Authors Library; the
American holdings (printed materials only) seem quite complete, but to date the collection is lacking in foreign editions
or translations.

Less work has been done in the area of secondary material.   Existing checklists are extremely selective, repeti-
tive, for the most part lack annotation and organization, and
offer an exceedingly limited, white academic perspective for
the consideration of Ellison's work.   The longest and most
useful of these checklists appears in Darwin T. Turner,
Afro-American Writers (1970), with coverage up to about
1968.   In general, the list by Nancy Tischler in Louis D.
Rubin, ed. , A Bibliographical Guide to the Study of Southern
Literature (1969), overlaps with Turner's, as does that in
Lewis Leary, ed. , Articles on American Literature 1950-1967
(1970).   Shorter critical references appear in Seymour L.
Gross and John E. Hardy, eds. , Images of the Negro in

American Literature (1966), and James A. Emanuel and
Theodore L. Gross, eds., Dark Symphony (1968). Equally
selective, but covering a period up to 1970, are the references in BlackW (December, 1970), in Donald B. Gibson,
ed., Five Black Writers (1970), and in John M. Reilly's
Twentieth Century Interpretations of "Invisible Man" (1970).

        Although the above checklists render an important
service in pointing the student to articles in major journals,
they suffer from the limitation of recording primarily the
white reader's confrontation with I. M.  As an example, although reviews in the white press are excluded from formal
checklists, they are copiously excerpted or quoted in many
of the most frequently used reference sources, whereas no
attempt is made there to seek out and record material from
the Afro-American press.  And while it is true that, until
recently, few black critics were welcomed in academic
journals, there does exist from the beginning a small body
of black critical opinion on Ellison which is usually ignored
in secondary checklists.  Now that neither the expression of
literary opinions nor the preparation of reference tools is
any longer the exclusive preserve of white scholarship, this
situation will, hopefully, soon be remedied.  In this connection, Ernest Kaiser's bibliographic essay, "A Critical
Look at Ellison's Fiction and at Social and Literary Criticism
by and about the Author" (BlackW, December, 1970), though
bearing obvious marks of the author's Marxist allegiances,
provides a perspective that is both impeccable in erudition
and sorely needed for its corrective value.  The recent development of a large body of black scholarship on Ellison
(as evidenced in part by the special issues on him in both
CLAJ and BlackW in 1970), gives further promise of a
more balanced treatment of materials in future library tools.

## III.  PRINCIPAL REVIEWS

a.  Invisible Man

This first novel by a hitherto relatively obscure writer received spectacular attention upon its publication: it was reviewed almost simultaneously by Saturday Review, New York Times Book Review, New York Times, New York Herald Tribune Book Review, Time, and New Republic, with other reviews following within a few months.  Perhaps this sheer bulk in itself accounts for the impression that the book elicited unanimous raves; curiously, the impression persists, even after one notes the fairly general technical criticism directed at the novel:  stylistically, the critics point to overwritten passages, verbosity, "artiness," and expressionistic obscurity:  the novel's tone is criticized as melodramatic, sometimes hysterical; excessive allegory and symbolism are also frequent complaints.  Structural criticism is rarer:  Delmore Schwartz (PR, May-June, 1952) notes that the book is almost all climax, while structural incoherence is pointed out by both George Mayberry (NR, April 21, 1952) and Irving Howe (Nation, May 10, 1952).  Despite all these flaws, endorsement seems to be overwhelming and, in many cases, in exaggerated terms:  "a hyperbole that represents most men" (Harvey C. Webster, SR, April 12, 1952); "blazes with authentic talent" (Orville Prescott, NYT, April 16, 1952); "sensational entry by the Negro into high literature" (William Barrett, Mercury, June, 1952).  The book is, in general, praised for its complexity and variety, for good storytelling, vividness, power, and humor.  Nonetheless, one must take exception to Ronald Gottesman's overindulgent assessment that "even at the beginning of its career, Invisible Man was understood to be specially pertinent to the history, condition and art of black Americans and, at the same time, to spring from and participate in broader themes and traditions" (Studies in Invisible Man, 1971).  Such an understanding is at this period given to a mere handful of readers; on the whole, it is

11

disturbingly clear that I. M. is not taken seriously on either
of these two planes, let alone on one which would render
them mutually interdependent.  Racism for example, surely
an issue of some moment in the total American reality, is
ignored in discussions of I. M.  The myopia is such that it
allows disregard of this problem, even when the book's
theme is actually spelled out:  says Milton S. Byam (LJ,
April 15, 1952):  "Negroes, in America, are 'invisible
men,'" following this with the comment that "the author dramatizes an interesting theme" (emphasis mine), a somewhat
less than total engagement with the implications of racial
prejudice.  Given this rather widespread phenomenon, a
brief discussion of the various critical strategies which en-
able the core of the novel to escape consideration might be
in order.

Some writers bypass the theme simply by ignoring
it and pointing to the book's optimism (Wright Morris,
NYT Book Review, April 13, 1952); or by hoping that the
author "will some day emerge from the underground to write
of other places" (George Mayberry, NR), as though it were
merely a question of thematic choice.

Esthetic considerations also serve as a shield from
reality:  the content is obscured by discussions of the manner of its expression, or by attempts to place the author
within a literary hierarchy:  Wright Morris (NYT Book Review) points out Ellison's mastery of anger; Harvey C. Webster (SR) states that the book puts Ellison among the "peers
of the best white writers of our day," while for William Barrett (Mercury) the book "just misses greatness" by failing
to provide alternatives to invisibility--not because such alternatives are obviated by the reality of racial prejudice,
but because Ellison fails to reach Dostoevski's "level of
richer and deeper human perception"!  Other reviewers are
prevented by "poor writing" from confronting the whole book;
both James Yaffe (YR, Summer, 1953), and Anthony West
(New Yorker, May 31, 1952), unhesitatingly advise the reader to skip some key passages in order to avoid undue labor.

The emphasis on esthetic criteria as almost self-
sufficient is underlined by the citation honoring Ellison with
the National Book Award (conferred in 1953 by the white book
trade).  Here the author is praised for his courage in taking
literary risks and in breaking away from conventional patterns of writing.  But no mention concerning the nature of
the work accomplished by means of those literary risks is

made; the essence, the probing exploration into the malfunc-
tioning American myth--surely a service of some cultural as
well as esthetic moment--is ignored in favor of the external
formal shell.  Compare this evasion with the outspoken approach of the black National Newspaper Publishers' Association which, also in 1953, confers its Russwurm Award upon
Ellison.  The award is given "for outstanding achievement
in making possibly a richer conception of democratic principles" and I. M. qualifies, because it has "shed new light
on the American problem of racism" (NYT, March 15, 1953).
Evidently, however, this new light is somewhat less than
generally diffused.

The concept of "universality" offers another avenue by
which the novel's very specific applicability is effectively de-
fused.  The very terms in which the novel is often praised
as "not just a protest novel, " or "not just about Negroes, "
allow the reviewer to note even its anger and bitterness without being disturbed, since their meaning is broadened into
a vague general abstraction.  The protagonist may even be
called "a Negro rebel" without arousing topical concern,
since his search is conveniently deflected toward "a universal statement of man's condition in our time" (NYT, January
31, 1953).

Conversely, the white reader is just as often prevented from seeing the relevance of the novel to himself,
by being told that it deals with the "limited" (i. e. , peripheral) category of Negro subject matter.  Most people would
take this to mean that its interest is primarily sociological,
and its tone probably restricted to one of rage and/or despair.  (As recently as 1971, Alfred Kazin still describes
what he terms the "best" black voice as one rising from
a wailing wall--"the gifted, unbearably frustrated man crying out for life, for more and more access to life, " SR,
October 2, 1971. )  James Yaffe (YR) praises "passages of
very great sociological interest"; Orville Prescott (NYT)
recommends it to anyone "interested in books by or about
Negroes" (emphasis mine); oblivious to irony, Time (April 14,
1952) hails the concept of self-fulfillment for every man,
and relegates Ellison to the position of "best of all U. S.
Negro writers. "  Worth T. Hedden (NYHT Book Review,
April 13, 1952) has the best of both worlds, universal and
particular, when he calls the book an Odyssey and yet
recommends it to anyone "interested in Negro-white relations in the depression decade. "  Thus, all too often, it
would appear that the book is praised because it allows

critics to discuss it without confronting it on a concrete
level.    Despite the fanfare and the encomiums, it is not the
book's meaning which is illuminated, but the failure of much
white critical sensibility.

There are, however, some notable exceptions:  Irving
Howe's review (Nation, May 10, 1952), despite its left-wing
perspective, addresses itself directly to two core issues
raised by I.M., namely the radical isolation of white from
black, and the difficulty of devising viable alternatives to
invisibility, given present social conditions.   T.E. Cassidy
(Commonweal, May 2, 1952) discusses the paradoxes and
contradictory behavior patterns afflicting him who is invisible.   R.W.B. Lewis (HudR, Spring, 1953) comments
along similar lines, and in addition is very suggestive in
describing the book's specific qualities of range and variety.
Richard Chase (KR, Autumn, 1952) succinctly hints at the
novel's depth--it "shows far more knowledge of mystery, suffering, transcendent reality, and the ultimate contractions of
life than most of the modern novels...." (p. 679).    Particularly impressive is Saul Bellow's review in Commentary
(June, 1952), though he, too, minimizes (or universalizes)
the race issue.   Welcoming I.M. as the sequel to the Battle Royal excerpt he had read "with great excitement" in
Horizon magazine, he is enthusiastic about the book's extraordinary maturity and integrity:

> ... one is accustomed to expect excellent novels
> about boys, but a modern novel about men is ex-
> ceedingly rare.   For this enormously complex and
> difficult American experience of ours very few
> people are willing to make themselves morally and
> intellectually responsible.   Consequently maturity
> is hard to find.  (p. 608)

While the book is not faultless (e.g., the Brotherhood episode), it is "immensely moving" and proves that "a truly
heroic quality can exist among our contemporaries ...",
i.e., those who "resist the heavy influences and make their
own synthesis out of the vast mass of phenomena ... to
rescue what is important" and to make by their tone "a
declaration of values" (p. 608).   Such a rare direct confrontation with the book's specifically American historic and
moral context surely comes closest to reflecting Ellison's
own terms of reference.

In searching for the reactions of black critics, one

finds that in many cases they have remained within the obscurity of the Afro-American press or of little magazines. Less numerous than their white counterparts, these readers through their particular approach nonetheless provide a much needed counterperspective upon the novel.

Contrary extremes are included in the range of black comments: sometimes the writer finds nothing to say, merely noting the novel's acclaim by the established white critics (Crisis, March, 1953; Negro History Bulletin, May, 1953). On the other hand, there is the scathing denunciation expressed by black critics of the Left, such as Abner W. Berry (The Worker, June 1, 1952), Lloyd L. Brown (Masses and Mainstream, June, 1952), John Oliver Killens (Freedom, June, 1952). Their arguments, marred by stridency and by almost formulaic homogeneity, accuse Ellison of distorting the Communist Party, vilifying Negro characters, disdaining the Negro masses, being pretentiously "arty," and adhering to the formula of "sex, sadism and anti-Communist clichés," for the sake of commercial success. As we shall see, some of these arguments are still around twenty years later, their passion unabated. (Sex aroused the concern of at least one other reader. Writing in the Pittsburgh Courier [April 4, 1953], P. L. Prattis complains that despite the book's obvious worth, he has removed it from his home, due to its gratuitous use of profanity, obscenity and filth.)

A very few black critics express wholehearted approval, albeit with technical reservations: Langston Hughes finds I. M. to be "deep, beautifully written, provocative and moving" (New York Age, February 28, 1953). Both Henry Winslow (Crisis, June-July, 1952) and Alain Locke in a more extensive essay (Phylon, 1953), praise the novel's artistic qualities, and, above all, its psychological realism, depth and skillful irony. They also point to the same defects, aptly summed up in Locke's words as "hyperbole and verbosity." Nevertheless, Locke unequivocally declares the novel to mark the third peak in the development of Negro fiction (following upon Cane, 1923, and Native Son, 1940).

But, for the most part, precisely the elements of artistic accomplishment and of truth are seriously questioned by black readers, in arguments that sometimes differ only in degree and temperance from those of the Leftist critics. Artistically speaking, Gertrude Martin (Chicago Defender, April 19, 1952) is disappointed in the novel compared to the

earlier short stories.  Neither characters nor situations
come to life, the treatment of women and of whites lacks
depth, and the whole reads like a case history.  Saunders
Redding objects (Afro-American, May 10, 1952) to a lack
of control and to a huge disproportion between the basic idea
that one must be oneself and its treatment:  "It is as if a
steam shovel were used to dig a compost pit for a kitchen
garden. "

Even more serious strictures are made about the
novel's truth.  Roi Ottley (Chicago Sunday Tribune, May 11,
1952) questions its apparent stress on the negative aspects
of black experience:  "I doubt that every Negro's life is only
an endless series of defeats and frustrations. "  Lucymae
Smith in the New York Age (April 26, 1952) utterly rejects
the portrayal of Negro life as unrealistic, "made in Hollywood, " and largely stereotyped.  In part these arguments
are residual legacies of the strong middle-class bias so often
deplored by black scholars, which consistently resists any depiction of lower-class black characters as prejudicial to the
cause of Negro advancement.  (See for example Sterling A.
Brown, "Our Literary Audience, " Opportunity, February,
1930, 42-46+. )  Marguerite D. Cartwright (Amsterdam News,
March 7, 14, 1953) facetiously entitles one of her two reviews "SPDNM" to stand for the "Society for the Prevention
of the Defamation of Negro Males, " but she is extremely
serious in accusing both Wright and Ellison of such defamation.  Her argument is supported by a reader, Florence
Murray (Amsterdam News, March 28, 1953), who points
out that works dealing with "normal" Negroes are neither
accepted nor publicized as I. M. was.  She suggests, indeed,
that I. M. 's success is partly due to its portrayal of Negroes
in line with acceptable stereotypes of Negro inferiority.

In sum, it might be said that I. M. did not reach its
audience on first impact; many black readers and critics
accepted it with deep reservations; and it failed to provoke
far-reaching personal or cultural self-examination in the
white circles where it was so enthusiastically hailed.  Indeed, the bulk of the reviews directly contradicts Granville
Hicks's assertion (SR, October 24, 1964) that "the day Invisible Man appeared, American culture was changed forever. "

b.   Shadow and Act (hereafter referred to as S & A)

Published in 1964, twelve years after I. M. , S & A

received immediate, though not quite as prolific attention as
I. M., particularly among white critics.  The book was, to
some, less welcome than a second novel would have been;
some felt that it was inferior, both to I. M. and to the essay-
style achieved by Baldwin.  The writing is often criticized
as poor, repetitious, and humorless.  Some reviewers (e. g.,
Granville Hicks, SR, October 24, 1964) frankly use S & A
as an adjunct to I. M.  But, on the whole, one is struck with
an apparently new critical willingness to attend to the matter
and manner of this book.  If there is a common theme to the
responses, it involves the expression of profound respect for
Ellison's integrity, intelligence and seriousness.  In part,
this betokens real progress in knowledgeable awareness in
the wake of the Civil Rights struggles.  It will also be re-
membered, however, that S & A appeared during a period
best described in the title of John A. Williams' 1962 book,
The Angry Black, or, as Newsweek put it, at a time when
"the subject of the Negro writer in America has explosive
and far-reaching implications" (August 24, 1964).  For many
of those shaken and angered by the denunciatory passion of
Malcolm X, James Baldwin or LeRoi Jones, Ellison's urbanity is in itself sufficient cause for praise.  The reviewer
who recommends S & A for college libraries "as an antidote
to the more hysterical proclamations coming from the pens
of James Baldwin and LeRoi Jones" (Choice, 1965) is fairly
representative; the adjective "sane" for S & A occurs with
significant frequency in most reviews, even when no explicit
reference to "the militants" is made.  Significantly, the
issue of activism in the arts, centering around the Ellison-
Howe debate as represented partly by the essay "The World
and the Jug" in S & A, receives a disproportionate amount of
attention, to the detriment of the other major theme in
S & A--the autonomy of black culture within a pluralistic
American context.  (Touching the Ellison-Howe debate,
Howe's viewpoint is generally dismissed out of hand, but
see Richard Chase's review in HR, 1965 for a more balanced
presentation. )

    That Ellison's refusal to admit proscription of the
artist's range applies with equal force to white stereotyping
("we want them [black writers] to be warriors, and wounded
warriors at that, " comments R. W. B. Lewis in the NY Review of Books) and to black militancy is a fact recognized
by the more perceptive critics.  Such stubborn resistance to
conditioning forces is "in itself, a school for the imagination
and moral sympathy" (Robert Penn Warren, Commentary,
May, 1965), worthy of emulation as a model of personal

integrity and wholeness.    "Hopefully," comments Elizabeth
Janeway (Christian Science Monitor, December 24, 1964),
"if we are lucky, civilization [in the twenty-first century]
will have ground along far enough to do for an elite what
Ellison has done for himself...." For readers such as
R. W. B. Lewis, Ellison's orientation even brings a sharpen-
ing of self-awareness as well as a new insight into the meaning of pluralism:

> Ellison's identity, because of the power, wisdom
> and stubborn sanity of its pronouncement, serves
> to limit mine, to establish its boundaries and focus
> its intermixing elements ... for Ellison is not only
> a self-identifier, but the source of self-definition
> in others.   At just that point, a falsely conceived
> integration (the melting of indistinguishable per-
> sons) ceases, and the dialogue can begin.

Some readers, on the other hand, remain unconvinced
by what they consider the book's excessive idealism.   Peter
de Lissovoy (Nation, November 9, 1964) notes the difficulty
for a black person in reconciling the Civil Rights struggle
with the possibility of total artistic self-fulfillment within
the status quo.   (The difficulty manifests itself aptly in the
conclusion George P. Elliott draws from S & A--that "it
is worse to be misconceived than to be oppressed," NYT
Book Review, October 25, 1964.)   Paul Velde (Commonweal,
February 19, 1965) argues that one cannot take a progressive view of history, that the Renaissance age of ideal-ful-
fillment is over, and that style and craft may serve too
easily as a shield against society, while Bell G. Chevigny
(Village Voice, November 19, 1964) points out with some
truth that S & A's implication that one merely needs to
grow up in order to fulfill one's ideals seems to be dis-
regarding the bitter lessons to the contrary learned at such
cost by the protagonist of I. M.

Comparatively little is said by the reviewers about
the relevance of Ellison's reflections on Negro culture as
both autonomous and contributory to American culture.   Indeed, the reviewer in Choice finds Ellison's assertions on
this subject "hyperbolic" and at times absurd, while Norman
Podhoretz (Book Week, October 25, 1964) suggests that,
possibly, the price of any minority's acceptance is the sur-
render of its subculture, and that the Negro "subculture"
might well find itself in the position of having to follow this
historically established pattern.   Elizabeth Janeway's com-

prehensive and thoughtful remarks on the subject probably
come closest to approach Ellison on his own ground.

Somewhat surprisingly, S & A was ignored by the
majority of black critics.   Miles M. Jackson mentions it
in the yearly survey of "Significant Belles-Lettres by and
about Negroes Published in 1964" (Phylon, Fall, 1965).
Hoyt W. Fuller predictably attacks it in a brief, satirical
mock-review (ND, August, 1965).   Here the integrity praised
by white critics is deplored as wrongheaded "universalism, "
expressing itself in excessive communication to whites and
inaccessibility to blacks, charges which gain in intensity in
subsequent years.   Nonetheless, S & A has gradually established itself among knowledgeable readers as an essential
contribution, extensively read and quoted in various contexts
relating to Black, American and folklore studies.

## IV.  GENERAL ESTIMATES

### 1952-1964

Far from being a passing fad, the prominence achieved by Ellison through the extensive reviews of I. M. in 1952 and the National Book Award in 1953 quickly became the basis for a solid reputation.   Least helpful in analyzing the ingredients of this esteem, although they occasionally record its presence, are the literary reference works of the period.   The Oxford Companion to American Literature, 3rd edition, is noteworthy for the relatively early date of its Ellison inclusion (1956, with an enlarged entry in the 1965 edition), though it misleadingly describes I. M. as a naturalistic novel. A curious entry in Howard Mumford Jones's widely available Guide to American Literature and Its Backgrounds Since 1890 (1953, unchanged through the third edition in 1964), includes I. M. under the heading of "Neonaturalism" of which the Negro novel is said to constitute "an especially grim phase," since it expresses an "inevitable outburst of hatred against the white man." Another handbook, The Reader's Encyclopedia of American Literature (1962),  contrary to its announced format, neglects to provide a bibliography of primary and secondary materials in the Ellison entry; it also misinterprets the novel's ending, by stating that the protagonist harbors "no trace of forgiveness or even hope for the future."  (But, "Hope! Think! Endurance!" is what Carl Milton Hughes reads as the novel's praiseworthy parting message in The Negro Novelist [1953], p. 273.)

Turning to other sources, notably the many scattered references to Ellison in thoughtful discussions of the contemporary cultural scene, one learns that he is appreciated as an innovator, marking in Margaret Just Butcher's words "a new level of literary achievement in both style and conception" (The Negro in American Culture, 1956, p. 179). Though style and conception form an integral entity, it is primarily the latter which seems to account for the serious

20

consideration given to Ellison in some scholarly circles.
For Alfred Kazin (Harper's, October, 1959) it is Ellison's
powerful rendering of modern absurdity which is significant.
Leslie Fiedler (Love and Death in the American Novel,
1960) is impressed by the skill with which form (the neo-
gothic) was put to the task of conveying absurdity in addition to the madness of race relations in America:   "to discuss, " as he put it, "in the light of pure reason the Negro
problem in the United States is to falsify its essential mystery and unreality:   it is a gothic horror of our daily lives"
(p.  470). 1

        Two major essays by Philip Roth ("Writing Ameri-
can Fiction, " Commentary, March, 1961) and R. W. B. Lewis
("American Letters:  a Projection, " YR, December, 1961)
explore even broader avenues.   Roth approves what he interprets as Ellison's repudiation of the unsuitably "bouncy"
tone of affirmation prevailing in a contemporary fiction whose
desperate retreat into self in truth offers no reason for celebration.   In response, Lewis amplifies Roth's critique with
some positive considerations:   singling out for praise some
promising qualities of postwar fiction, he links Ellison with
the best of these, thus broadening his contribution from one
of mere abstention to one of active moral and aesthetic in-
novation.   Ellison, like others who "directed their imagination and their daring to resisting those terrible twins, conformity and chaos, " has projected a new comic hero who
reflects our cultural needs.   What enhances this new hero-
type's moral significance is his stubborn "hanging on" to his
incipient sense of self, while also actively searching out-
ward for a moral order beyond himself.   This double quest
is an exploitation of our cultural predicament as well as a
courageous response to it:  and in Ellison and Purdy, Lewis
sees two writers who crystallize these issues in their work
and offer us a sort of "inverted order ... bright with paradox, " but ripe with human possibility.   This thesis is
further developed in Lewis' essay "Recent Fiction:  Picaro
and Pilgrim" (R. E. Spiller, ed. , A Time of Harvest,
1962), where the protagonists of Ellison, Bellow, Salinger,
Kerouac, Purdy and Mailer are discussed as not only rogues
and picaros, but also as "pilgrims journeying through a mysterious and hostile world ... toward some shrine of honor
and value and belief" (p. 149).

        The careful reader of Ellison will be struck by the
applicability to him of Lewis' general comments stressing
these writers' exploration of "the great sources of power

and control in our epoch" (p. 152), their "stubborn idio-
syncrasy of individuality, " and "deliberate vulnerability to
life" (p. 145). [2]  In a similar vein, Lewis' much earlier
study, The American Adam (1955), though it deals primarily
with nineteenth-century American writers, is remarkable for
the perspicacity of its comments on Ellison, among others,
in the book's closing pages.

Ellison also finds his place among the literary van-
guard in W. Thorp's brief references in American Writing
in the Twentieth Century (1960) and Malcolm Cowley's more
extensive discussion in The Literary Situation (1954), which
groups Invisible Man with Algren's Man With a Golden Arm
and Bellow's The Adventures of Augie March.  Here the
qualities of this literary vanguard--the strong affirmation of
the individual's value, the controlled, very modified use of
naturalistic technique, the courageous expression of convic-
tions in a time of general timidity--are all pointed out, together with the technical dangers inherent in such experi-
mentation.  (For comic relief one should mention a strangely
patronizing essay by S. Krim (PR, May-June, 1952), expressing his boredom with contemporary fiction for not keep-
ing up with the speed of his mind, but adding a postscript
in which he cites I.M. as the only recent American novel
trying to move in the proper direction, even though the book
itself is "raw and overambitious. ")

Though scattered and generalized, the estimates cited
above are notable on two counts--the breadth of their perspective, and the absence of black participants in these
broad cultural critiques of the American scene.  And while
breadth of perspective allowed, as we have noted, great
perspicacity in the assessment of Ellison's contribution, the
absence of black critical opinion is painfully felt in the many
instances where racial assumptions do intrude to limit the
outlook of white critics.  Here, operating strictly within the
separate, reduced category of "Negro literature" as distinct
from "Negro-American" literature, Ellison also ranks high--
Newsweek pronounces him and Baldwin as "our two most important Negro writers" (August 24, 1964).  But the grounds
for this eminence are as shallow as the classification itself,
resting primarily on Ellison's supposed repudiation of naturalism, protest writing, the Richard Wright school (and by
1964, the young militant writers' school).  Parochial as
these yardsticks for measuring achievement are, they are far
more common than the R.W.B. Lewis-Philip Roth approach.
From here it is only a short step down toward the patron-

izing tone.    Thus Bone's controversial estimate of I. M. as
"by far the best novel yet written by an American Negro, "
which usually obscures the latter part of his statement,
"quite possibly the best American novel since World War
II"; or Leon Howard's view that Ellison is the first to approach Van Vechten's (another white man's) hitherto unsur-
passed knowledge of Harlem (Literature and the American
Tradition, 1960).   Next one passes into the area of total
neglect:   surely it is racially conditioned assumptions which
dictate the exclusion of Ellison and other Negro writers from
consideration in such works as R.  E.  Spiller (The Cycle of
American Literature, 1955), Perry Miller et al. , eds. ,
Major Writers of America, 1962, and R.  W.  Stallman et
al. , eds. , American Literature, Readings and Critiques
(1961).

          In spite of the various and discouraging manifesta-
tions of Ellison's built-in invisibility, it is still possible to
conclude by focusing on the most compelling critical responses that he has indubitably achieved in this period a
place of solid prominence, resting mostly upon cultural
and esthetic rather than ideological-sociological considerations.


                              1965-1971

          Ellison's reputation has grown steadily during this
period, but this growth has been fraught with so much controversy that questions of artistic merit sometimes seem
all but forgotten amid the ideological, racial and political
motivations of his most vocal friends and detractors.    While
in the long run these polemics may recede into their proper
place as tokens of the aberrations of the time, they constitute for the moment the predominent characteristic of the
period under discussion, and thus need to be dealt with in
some detail.

          The period opens with the often cited New York
Herald Tribune Book Week poll taken in September, 1965,
in which 200 authors, critics and editors were asked to
assess the fiction of the twenty-year period 1945-1965;
Ellison ranks sixth in response to the question as to what
authors had written the most distinguished fiction, but I. M.
tops the list of the "20 best books" of the period.    Given
the exclusion of black intellectuals from the poll, its results amount to an adoption of Ellison by the white literary

establishment, a fact sufficient in itself to place him in a
false light in many quarters.   Other signs of Ellison's pres-
tige among academics are legion--numerous honorary doc-
torates, election to the National Institute of Arts and Letters, distinguished teaching appointments, the latest being
the Albert Schweitzer Professorship of the Humanities at
New York University in 1970.   On a less rarefied level,
college courses, an NET film, the growing number of dissertations, and a veritable landslide of articles (80 major
essays in the 65-71 period, as compared to 30 in 52-64)
bear further witness to his high standing.

It is not always easy to tell the serious from the
spurious attention, yet in the case of a reputation such as
Ellison's which strikes one as slightly inflated, the question
inevitably arises.   Are white readers fascinated with I. M.
because it allows them to impose on it their private racial
images and attitudes?  See for example F. W. Dupee's
highly favorable essay in the NYHT poll issue, in which he
praises the sense I. M. conveys to him of the prevailing
bleakness, loneliness, and pain of the black experience (the
very notions that Ellison has repeatedly argued against).
When Dupee describes I. M. as a praiseworthy attempt at
"the humanization of the Negroes by linking their history ...
with the history ... of mankind at large ... "3 is not his
perception of it at some distance from Ellison's expressed
purpose, namely that he "felt it important to explore the
full range of American Negro humanity" ("That Same Pain
... , " S & A, p. 36)?  (Emphasis mine. )  If even a sympathetic white reader "may mean good, but he do' so doggone
po'" as the Negro folk saying goes, one may well be concerned as to when and by what means such a fundamental
gulf in perceptions might be bridged.   There is, in any
event, some justification for contentions such as Gayle Addison Jr. 's (ND, January, 1967) that Ellison's popularity
is attributed in large measure to the ability of the critics to
deal with him while avoiding his skillfully disguised indictment of American society.  Darwin T. Turner, another black
critic, has on many occasions suggested that it is Ellison's
accessibility to mythic and symbolic critical approaches
(another way of bypassing racial confrontation), which en-
dears him to followers of the New Criticism.   Even more
irrelevant reasons may come into play, such as "white guilt
and a desire to help the Negro" suggested by David Madden
(ER, April, 1968), and approval of Ellison's politics--his
refusal, as John V. Hagopian put it, to be "mau-maued" by
the "black militants and their radical chic dupes" into

accepting the rhetoric of black cultural nationalism (SN, Summer, 1971). That the general level of discussion about Ellison has shifted to barren low ground at a great remove from the provocative breadth of the R. W. B. Lewis approach is regrettably clear from the tenor of much writing in this period. Note, for example, Hagopian's article which proceeds to berate Ellison for making a career of being a "professional good colored boy" and "muzzling himself politically in the name of good taste and manners in return for favors from the government and the conservative establishment. "

Hagopian's complaint also points to the crucial fact that Ellison, and the range of his potential for controversy, have moved considerably beyond academe: he is trustee of various organizations such as the New School for Social Research, the City Museum of New York, and that city's Educational Television station; appointed member of the twenty-five-man American Revolution Bicentennial Commission (1967), of a Ford Foundation Panel awarding grants for public affairs and educational television programs (1968), and recipient of the Freedom Medal, the highest civil award in the power of a President to bestow (1969). Inevitably, such pre-eminence heightens Ellison's artificial image as a white man's model Negro, raised up to stand as a comfortable bulwark against the intractable hostilities of the young militants. One curious example of this kind of wishful thinking is the episode of Ellison's testimony before a Senate Subcommittee investigating the crisis of the cities and of Harlem in 1966. By no stretch of the imagination can Ellison be described as offering "a view of the problem from the back street of the ghetto itself" (NYT, September 4, 1966); yet his testimony on life in Harlem was reported in great detail, with much stress on his urbanity and his quiet voice, even though his views were perhaps less adequate reflections of living conditions than those of more "uncouth" and loud actual residents of the area.

Regrettably, the interests of blacks and whites in our society do not yet coincide, nor is conciliation the watchword of the day. With both sides in desperate need of images, Ellison finds himself doubly exploited, for if subconscious white needs have cast him as the "good Negro, " equally urgent black needs have cast him correspondingly as a turncoat. Ironically enough, the major casualty of this shadow-boxing is the very subject which could have contributed to an authentic rapprochement--Ellison's endeavor "to explore the full range of American Negro humanity. To

be sure, this climate of discourse is not universal; nonetheless, characteristic black reactions to Ellison in this period
range from ambivalence to outright hostility.

        By and large, the estimate of Ellison found in Negro
reference works is ambivalent, or at least noncommittal.
He, along with Baldwin, is excluded entirely from Great
Negroes, 3rd ed. (1969), a textbook for use in white primary and secondary schools, published by Afro-Am in
Chicago. The Negro Handbook (1966), The Negro Almanac
(1967), and the International Library of Negro Life and
History (1968) merely note that he won acclaim for his
novel. In the latter work, his position is peripheral, compared to Wright and the younger writers. Arna Bontemps'
comments in The American Negro Reference Book (1966)
ring uneasily ambivalent when he describes Invisible Man as
"sculptured, " or speaks of Ellison's "a-novel-a-decade rate
of composition. "

        An essay by James Walker (Black Creation, 1970)
states some of the causes of current black dissatisfaction with
Ellison--his "vision of Black people as an integral part of
a society controlled by white" and his outdated "sense of
accommodation and willingness to try and change the prevalent white views"--but is careful to stress that in I.M.
Ellison is also offering a thorough condemnation of white
society "for its racial shortsightedness, its bigotry, its
viciousness" (p. 16). But most of the overt antagonism to
Ellison is less balanced. One line of resistance is Marxist
oriented, and Harold Cruse has skillfully traced in Crisis
of the Negro Intellectual (1967) the continuing leftwing attacks on Ellison since the publication of I.M. In the 1960's
we often find the older left ideology allying itself with neo-
Marxism and with cultural nationalism, to brand Ellison as
a traitor to the black cause or as simply irrelevant. A
large and growing amount of material has been generated
by these views, with most of the attacks appearing in the
pages of Negro Digest (now Black World), and climaxing
in 1967 and 1968. The hostility takes various interesting
forms: for example, John Henrik Clarke writes "The
Origin and Growth of Afro-American Literature" (ND, December, 1967) and omits Ellison's contribution entirely, by
simply skipping a decade: "Among black writers the period
of the 1940's was the period of Richard Wright. The period
of the 1960's was the period of James Baldwin" (p. 66).
More direct is Ernest Kaiser's indictment found in his
Freedomways review of Gross and Hardy's Images of the

Negro in American Literature:

> Ellison has become an Establishment writer, an
> Uncle Tom, an attacker of the sociological formula-
> tions of the civil rights movement, a defender of
> the criminal Vietnam war of extermination against
> the Asian (and American Negro) people, a denigra-
> tor of the great tradition of Negro protest writing
> and, worst of all for himself as a creative artist,
> a writer of weak and ineffectual fiction and essays
> mostly about himself and how he became an artist.
> (p. 157)

Kaiser included this paragraph without change in his longer
bibliographic essay on Ellison's writings and critics which
appeared three years later in the special BlackW Ellison
issue (December, 1970).   Returning to 1967, the "Perspectives" section of ND for August commented that "Ralph Ellison, surely one of the most gifted of American writers, is
rapidly losing his luster among black intellectuals even as
he gains in glitter in the white Establishment" (p. 49).
When, in January, 1968, ND ran its own book pool among
thirty-eight black writers, much was made editorially of the
fact that more than half the respondents named Richard Wright
as the most important black writer.   In point of fact, Langston Hughes, Ralph Ellison and James Baldwin followed
Wright very closely as second and third choices, but this
was definitely underplayed.   On the heels of this poll Clifford Mason wrote a piece published in Life for May, 1970,
wherein he explicitly set up Wright as an "authentic" black
writer in symbolic counterpoise to Ralph Ellison.

The ND poll seems to have been conceived as a ve-
hicle for the expression of principles animating the new
Black Arts movement, but careful reading of the printed
excerpts from the reactions shows that a large number of the
respondents actually expressed reservations and qualifications
about some of the poll's premises, especially on the question
of restricting black writers to black materials and to a black
audience.   Not much was said either attacking Ellison, but
no doubt Etheridge Knight's rejection of I. M. for appealing
to white readers is in line with the editorial feelings of the
journal.   Back in 1962, LeRoi Jones had already made a
similar point in his wholesale rejection of pre-nationalistic
Negro writing as assimilationist and lacking in quality as
well as in integrity:

... only Jean Toomer, Richard Wright, Ralph
Ellison and James Baldwin have managed to bring
off examples of writing, in this genre, that could
succeed in passing themselves off as 'serious'
writing, in the sense that, say, the work of Somer-
set Maugham is 'serious' writing. That is, serious, if one has never read Herman Melville or
James Joyce....

> (The Myth of a 'Negro Litera-
> ture', " 1962 address published
> in Home (New York, 1966),
> p. 107.)

Ellison's "assimilationism, " his lack of contact with
young black writers, and his delay in publishing his second
novel are also, singly or together, subject to criticism.
See Gayle Addison, Jr.'s 1970 essay, " The Function of
Black Literature at the Present Time, " in his The Black
Aesthetic (1972), or the verse satire, "Note From a Non-
Intellectual on Ralph Ellison (Commemorating the Non-Com-
pletion of his Second Novel), " in BlackW, April, 1971.
And the tone of Ellison's interviews gets increasingly defensive all through the late sixties, reflecting his awareness
of these various charges.   In 1970, various shadings of
black attitudes toward Ellison may be conveniently studied in
the two special Ralph Ellison numbers of CLAJ (March, 1970)
and BlackW (December, 1970).

Absorbing and well-publicized as the double image
game is, many non-participants can be found, for neither
white acclaim nor black denunciation are as monolithic as
one might suppose.   Black intellectuals such as Larry Neal,
Lance Jeffers, Nathan A. Scott, Stephen Henderson, James
Baldwin, Saunders Redding and Albert Murray, who have
given serious consideration to Ellison's work, come from
the young as well as the older generation.   Conversely,
white recognition of his artistic (as distinct from his sociological) value, is by no means a fait accompli.   I.M. may
have been number one in the Book Week poll, but when Jackson Bryer polled 182 scholars for suggestions about twentieth century authors to be included in his projected Fifteen
Modern American Authors, only two of them named Ralph
Ellison. 4  Up to August, 1973, he had not yet been elected
to the Modern Language Association's list of Honorary Fel-
lows.   (But the latest General Assembly in December, 1973
has just elected him an Honorary Fellow.)

   Similarly, if one examines the entries in white
authored reference works and literary histories, one will
still find scanty coverage, misinterpretation, and exclusion
from the larger American context.  Whereas Earl Rovit's
contribution to The Encyclopedia of World Literature in the
Twentieth Century (1967) is both informative and concise,
one notes with some wonder the approach taken as late as
1966 by W. Blair et al., eds., The Literature of the United
States, 3rd ed. (a history and anthology).  Here the focus
is extra-literary:  racial problems are dismissed with the
assurance that the Negro's allegiance to Christianity and
democracy is "probably an adequate safeguard against actual
insurrection" (p. 1347).  Within this framework, the advent
of Ellison and Baldwin is hailed as "encouraging for the
Negro cause" because of their "wide social impact" (p. 1348).
But it is suggested (after a capsule summary of I. M. which
states that the narrator fails to find an identity) that Ellison's
best work may yet lie in the future.  Some noteworthy ex-
clusions of Ellison should also be pointed out--notably from
such a widely used anthology of American literature as S.
Bradley et al., The American Tradition in Literature, 3rd
ed., 1967.  (The only black writer included in Volume II
of this anthology is LeRoi Jones, who is introduced with the
telling editorial comment that "race is not often an issue in
his poetry and does not restrict its appeal," p. 1721.)
Ellison is equally excluded from the company of other major American authors in such works as Arthur Mizener's
Twelve Great American Novels (1967).  Indeed, in some re-
spects, the later period seems to bring little improvement
in the quality of Ellison scholarship; this is especially evident when one compares Robert Bone's history of Negro
Literature with the much more superficial treatment of the
same topic by David Littlejohn (Black on White).  As late
as 1966, we find here a combination of superficiality and
facile judgment in Littlejohn's firm pigeonholing of Ellison
as "only the finest of American Negro novelists" (p. 118).

   The most careful assessment of Ellison to date has
been in two anthology textbooks restricted specifically to
black literature: Donald B. Gibson, ed., Five Black Writers
(1970) and James A. Emanuel and Theodore L. Gross, eds.,
Dark Symphony (1968).  The former discussion (in the editor's introduction) limits itself to I. M., but is trenchant,
and offers an inclusive perspective on problems as well as
qualities.  The latter (in the lengthy headnote to the Ellison
selections) is unique in its attempt to deal with Ellison's
achievement as an integral whole.  Its careful, balanced

integration of life, ideas, and creative output stands out as
a model for critical emulation.   Of course, Ellison is by
now widely anthologized in Afro-American texts, but not many
editors trouble to assess the reasons for their inclusion of
his work.

As a final index to the popularity of I. M. on the college level, one may cite the fact that by 1971 there exist at
least three study aid volumes on this book:   a volume in
the Twentieth Century Views series edited by John M.   Reilly
(1970), a Monarch Study Guide edited by Elizabeth C.   Phillips
(1971), and a volume in the Charles Merrill Studies, edited
by Ronald Gottesman (1971).

It can be said by the end of 1971 that Ellison is widely
read, taught, anthologized and written about, but that all
this attention notwithstanding, something is still lacking:   it
may be, as Donald Gibson suggests, that "none of us, it
seems, can get sufficiently far above [his work] to see it
truly in its entirety" (Five Black Writers, p. xix).   Yet
one does sense a slowly growing awareness of the central
nature of his concerns and of previous critical limitations
(esthetic, ideological or racial) in dealing with them.

Perhaps a period of critical hiatus and closer study
is most desirable at this point.   In any case, new evaluations
will have to be made out of a familiarity with Ellison's early
work, as well as from a thorough, non-partisan, understanding of his total artistic, cultural and racial stand, as
expressed in his fiction and nonfiction.   There need be no
haste whatever about allotting him a permanent niche within
any literary hierarchy; there is, however, an urgent need
to bring about a more general appreciation of his unique
contribution, which far exceeds the category of the merely
esthetic.   The entries in literary reference works will have
to be rewritten more carefully and inclusively.   Literary
histories will have to allot space and care to adequately
comprehensive discussions.   And special studies remain to
be written, assessing Ellison's impact on specific cultural
areas, and examining the revolutionary extraliterary scope
of his work, especially I. M.   Even casual reading reveals
Ellison to be gradually turning into a seminal figure--a
variety of persons, white as well as black, are discovering
him on their frequency, and reacting to his ideas while
clarifying their own.   Whether it be in music, in political
ideology, in racial self-definition, in letters, or in more
profoundly personal ways, the clarity and range of his

thinking are making themselves felt, and await proper study and greater dissemination.

# V. CRITICAL STUDIES

## 1952-1964

Since the publication of I. M. in 1952, Ellison has received steady critical attention, whose momentum has gradually built up. The bulk of the discussions is concerned with thematic and structural analysis.

I. M. invites general explication of meaning and elucidation of major structural and symbolic elements, but its very richness resists total analysis. The more helpful essays are those which do not attempt total inclusiveness. Jonathan Baumbach's discussion in Critique (Spring, 1963) is provocative in its interpretation of Tod Clifton as a martyr-saint and in its judgment that Ellison excels as a satirist and surrealist, but fails as a realist when he is "talky, didactic, even at times ... tedious. " J. Noel Heermance (ND, May, 1964) isolates what he considers Ellison's two major innovations in the tradition of the Negro novel: 1) his "harsh and frank description" of the roles available to Negroes within the "Cage" of white society, and 2) his use of the Negro culture to show how these roles may be transcended. A similar point is stressed within a different context by Morris Beja--"It Must Be Important: Negroes in Contemporary American Fiction, " AR (Fall, 1964), pp. 323-336. An essay by Ellin Horowitz, On Contemporary Literature, ed. R. Kostelanetz (1964), is too broad to be helpful; by bringing together everything from the blues to Frazer, Freud, and Joyce, it produces confusion, superficiality, forced parallels, undeveloped points and inconsistency. In contrast, Robert Bone's discussion (The Negro Novel in America, 1958) succeeds in being both informative and comprehensive, though one might not always agree with some of his statements.

Much writing has been devoted to the study of special motifs and symbols in I. M. Rather surprisingly, however,

the dynamic role played by Negro folk culture within the
novel receives little in-depth study in this period.  It has
been charged, with some justice, that white critics were
unable to go beyond I. M. 's existential and mythic dimensions because of their ignorance of the black experience
(Joyce Nower, NALF, Spring, 1969).  But with the exception of James Baldwin[5] neither do the black readers in this
period seem more alert to additional dimensions in this
novel.  Whereas Robert Bone, a white scholar, points to
Ellison's "vision of the possibilities of Negro life" through
its cultural resources, the late Arna Bontemps seems to
ignore this component of the book altogether.  He stresses
Ellison's overriding interest in craftsmanship, but in speaking of "that tenet of the New Criticism which rules out folk
themes and sociological questions as proper materials for
serious art" he neither recognizes nor credits the many
ways in which Ellison bypasses that tenet, especially with
respect to folk themes (in W. Griffin, ed. , Literature in
the Modern World, 1954).  It is, in point of fact, mainly
white readers who approach the subject at all, even if in-
adequately:  Stanley Hyman is one of the first to identify
such Negro folk motifs as archetypal folk figures, use of the
Negro sermon tradition, and of the blues (PR, Spring, 1958).
His interpretation of these motifs, particularly of the folk
figures in the novel, is, however, so general that Ellison
himself objected to it (in the same issue of PR; see also
S & A, pp. 61-73).  Noel Heermance, as already mentioned, points to the positive use of Negro folk culture as
a major achievement, but he gives this no further analysis.
Use of the Brer Bear and Brer Rabbit motifs is studied by
Floyd R. Horowitz (MASJ, Fall, 1963), but the discussion
lacks the sense of a felt folk tradition.  Bone's comments
on I. M. (The Negro Novel in America, 1958) also touch in
a general way upon the stylistic folk resources of which
Ellison took advantage.  In view of the foregoing, it is no
surprise to find Ellison as late as 1960 still working to ex-
pound the notion that a distinctive, rich, Negro American
culture has been created in this country, that it is totally
separate from the cultures of Africa, and that it is in need
of appreciative recognition (Harold R. Isaacs, Phylon, Winter, 1960).

     To be sure, many white readers are ignorant at this
time of black folk culture, or too convinced of the totally
negative character of the black experience to believe in the
existence of positive elements within it.  Thus Alfred Maund
(CJF, Fall, 1954) uses I. M. in partial support of the

argument that "there is no Negro culture, as such, in
America.... Where the Negro is excluded, he builds his
own society, but it is a hollow, shallow image of that from
which he is barred" (p. 34). But, as noted, nothing written
by black critics at this time compels one to more informed
attitudes.

The sociological perspective is stressed by Nick
Aaron Ford, one of the few black critics discussing I. M.
in this period (Phylon, March, 1954). His essay compares
Wright, Ellison, Motley and Yerby, and while conceding Ellison's stature as a major writer, he finds him "deficient
in feeling," distorting reality in a "flight toward fantasy"
comparable to Yerby's "flight toward romance," and con-
fused in straddling the tragic and comic genres. On this
last point, Norman Mailer would seem to agree. In his
capsule evaluation of Ellison in Advertisements For Myself
(1959), he criticizes Ellison for "forever tumbling from the
heights of pure satire into the nets of a murderously de-
pressed clown," a weakness due in Mailer's view to insufficient control over his "rage, horror, and disgust." (En-
ter here the stereotyped notion regarding the staples of the
Negro writer's craft.) As we shall see, it is precisely the
tragicomic tone which later readers will single out as a
major ingredient of I. M.'s richness.

A rare contribution from German scholarship, Ursula Brumm's "The Figure of Christ in American Literature" (PR, 1957), analyzes the unique tragic outlook which
use of the Adam-Christ typology introduces into the work
of American writers from Melville through Ellison.

Other symbols and motifs studied in this period include the use of the Negro college in I. M. as a protest
symbol--Juanita G. Starke, Phylon (December, 1956), and
the use of the symbolism of vision--Charles I. Glicksberg,
SWR (1954); this study appears to offer the conclusion that
the locus of the racial problem is within the Negro's mind.

The incest motif (the Trueblood-Norton episode) is
discussed from the vantage point of a practicing psychiatrist
by Selma Fraiberg, PR (September-October, 1961). Align-
ing this episode with other modern literary treatments of
the motif, the writer concludes that significant new attitudes
toward the incest myth seem to be emerging among contemporary writers. Her interpretation also has specific
pertinence to the novel's central preoccupation with the process of illusion-stripping.

The thematic discussions, which also abound in this period, have centered mostly on the theme of the search for identity.  W. Tasker Witham's study, The Adolescent in the American Novel (1964), discusses the invisible protagonist's experiences within the broader context suggested by the title.  Wilbur M. Frohock, in Strangers to This Ground (1961), feels that Ellison's hero in his running illustrates the Great American Topos that "the image of the American hero of our time is the image of a D. P." (p. 9). (Cf. also discussions of the running image in John H. Randall, III, RLV, 1965, and Phyllis R. Klotman, CLAJ, March, 1970).  But Richard Pearce (MR, 1964), using Lewis' "Picaro and Pilgrim" essay as his point of departure, sees the best of the protagonists of contemporary fiction as illustrating the key idea of Thoreau's "Walking"--at home anywhere, in search of the Holy Land, but not concerned with goals or roles, nor judging the world, but telling their stories from a mature perspective.  Most of the other thematic "identity" studies of I. M. stress the problematic nature of the novel's ending.  Thus, Floyd Horowitz, CLAJ (December, 1963), is disturbed at the hero's agreement to a continuing confusion between good and evil, when the novel's whole development has seemed to promise his emergence as a rationalist.

There is also disagreement as to the degree to which the ending shows the protagonist accepting his black identity; but there seems to be unspoken agreement to the effect that such an identity is either insufficient or counterproductive for the protagonist, as well as for society.  Steven Marcus, Commentary (November, 1953), praises Ellison's "unapologetic relish for the concrete richness of Negro living," and sees the protagonist as unique in "rushing to his Negro identity," but concludes nonetheless that these are mere salvage operations, the Negro writer being compelled to wrest from his narrow world links to unite him with Western man, in an ever more anxious quest "to discover his kinship with the white race and with human history."  Howard Levant, MASJ (Fall, 1963), goes even further:  because Ellison leaves his hero in a "comic" predicament at the end, he is said to imply that "it is not possible to take the Negro seriously at the present time."

Indeed, the novel's humor is a neglected subject in this period.  With very few exceptions (notably Alain Locke and Earl H. Rovit), most readers of I. M. didn't really think--to paraphrase Ellison's query to an interviewer--that

the book was at all funny.   Among black critics, those who
did note the humor either objected to it, as did Nick Aaron
Ford, or simply enjoyed it without analysis, as did Alain
Locke; whereas Russell A. Brooks, seeing the novel as "in
dead earnest" when satirizing the foibles of blacks, uses it
in partial evidence of his contention that the Negro "has yet
to learn how to laugh at his own follies" ("The Comic Spirit
and the Negro's New Look, " CLAJ, September, 1962, p. 43).

     Other structural and thematic approaches to the end-
ing draw negative conclusions about its redemptive possibilities.   Marcus Klein, After Alienation (1964), reads the
novel's circular structure as underlining the protagonist's
inevitable failure to achieve identity (visibility).   Not only
does he see this structure as contradicting the "desperate"
optimism of the novel's ending, but also as suggesting a
quite different resolution--namely, the hero's acceptance
of a permanent outsider's role, and his embrace of a satan-
ic identity which will, henceforth, brood destructively over
civilization (a sort of Bigger-Thomas-as-philosopher).   In
a different context but with equal pessimism, Leslie Fiedler,
in Love and Death in the American Novel (1960 and revised
1966 edition), praises I. M. 's neo-gothic form as particularly suited to expressing the violent and absurd world of
modern existence and black-white relations in America.
Unlike R. W. B. Lewis, Richard Lehan, TSLL (Summer,
1959), sees the invisible man as yet another contemporary
hero "unable to redeem himself from a fallen world, a
modern hell" (p. 195).

     Another existentialist and basically hopeless reading
is offered by Esther M. Jackson, Phylon (Winter, 1962).
Comparing the protagonist with Bigger Thomas and Joe
Christmas, Jackson finds him to have reached the highest
stage of existential rebellion--a rebellion characterized,
however, merely by a Sisyphus-like mental illumination of
his suffering.   While such a posture may be valid for all
men on a strictly metaphysical basis, it strikes one as
inapplicable to I. M. 's world, where the roots of suffering
are neither immutable nor exclusively metaphysical.   The
abstraction of the purely existential analysis is offset by
the exchange between Irving Howe and Ellison in the pages
of Dissent (Autumn, 1963) and the New Leader (February
3, 1964), which prefigures many of the later ideological
arguments surrounding I. M. and its author.   Here some
very concrete issues are forcefully aired:  whether the
Negro can become visible in our society; the ramifications

of his invisibility; what, practically, constitutes a black
identity and how it may best be expressed; what is the ultimate nature and aim of art.    The debate, unfortunately,
hardens into a rigid ideological dispute, both protagonists
taking up extreme positions and refusing to budge.    Howe
persists in setting up allegedly incompatible categories of
"humanity" versus "art"; Ellison is equally insistent in re-
jecting this distinction as spurious and as a threat to his
human and artistic integrity.    This inconclusive deadlock
sets the keynote to much critical consideration of Ellison
in the next period.

## 1965-1971

According to John Hagopian, Invisible Man "needs no
critic to unravel its meaning, for the narrator clearly articulates it in his final commentary" (Studies in the Novel,
Summer, 1971).    But word of their redundancy has yet to
reach the critics:    when James Justus writes in his 1969
American Literary Scholarship essay that "Ellison and
Malamud are subjects of more articles than at any time in
the past, " he is noting a trend which shows no signs of
abating yet.    Almost three times as many essays on Ellison
have been written in the last six years (1965-1971) as in the
preceding twelve year period (1952-1964).

As before, the bulk of the criticism deals with I. M.
Inevitably, much of this material represents facile duplication; yet some vital new perspectives have also been added,
notably a significant increase in the number of black
scholars addressing themselves to Ellison's work, frequent
drawing upon the S & A essays for elucidation of Ellison's
ideas, a far more detailed exploration of the various dimensions of blackness in the novel, concurrent with sharper
awareness of its distinctive American qualities; and more
dynamic interpretations of the novel's ending, which was
earlier judged as static, if not negative.

Of great moment also is the changed context for
these studies, namely the more "explosive" character of
contemporary race relations and the far more acrimonious
relations between Ellison and portions of the black intellectual community discussed in the preceding section.    These
changes account for the frequent intrusion of the personal
and the polemic into "academic" appraisals.

Theme, imagery, symbolism

        This heading accounts once more for the largest body
of criticism.  Image, metaphor and symbol analysis still
appears as a fertile avenue:  the centrality of sight is discussed by Alice Bloch (EJ, November, 1966), while Darwin
T. Turner focuses on the neglected aspect of this theme--
the narrator's own inability to see (CLAJ, March, 1970).
In the same special Ellison issue of CLAJ, Phyllis R. Klotman discusses the Running Man as a major fictional figure
of black and American tradition, noting that Ellison's Running
Man reflects both the negative and the positive aspects of
this tradition, while epitomizing the experience of black and
white in the twentieth century.   James Walker (Black Creation, Summer, 1970), argues that the machine (in the literal sense, and as a symbol of white racism) is the neglected
controlling metaphor of the entire novel.  Lloyd W. Brown
(SBL, September, 1970), discusses among others Ellison's
highly conscious use of names "as the center of a network
of symbolic implications" and as a means of unexpected
transfiguration, seeing this as an approach typical to African
thinking.

        The sexual theme is dealt with in two articles.
Peter L. Hays argues that incest in the novel functions
paradigmatically as an exploitative set of relationships between people (WHR, Autumn, 1969).   Frederick L. Radford suggests (JAmS, February, 1971) that the novel's unevenness is largely the result of uneven success in treating
the sex theme--Ellison succeeds in showing the ways in
which black sexual identity is stereotyped and exploited,
but his effort to turn from defense to attack by offering the
black stereotype of the lustful white woman is unconvincing.
(For a general discussion of the literary uses of sex see
Marian E. Musgrave, "Triangles in Black and White:  Interracial Sex and Hostility in Black Literature," CLAJ 14,
no. 4, June, 1971, 444-451. )

        The identity theme elicits varied responses.  Russell
W. Nash reads I. M. as an exposition and counterstatement
to political, economic and social stereotypes (SQ, Autumn,
1965).   L. Lee and William J. Schafer explore the "proper
self" sought by the protagonist and his use of the anti-hero
and of the Sambo stereotype respectively (Descant, Spring,
1966 and Critique, 1968).  Most provocative is Eleanor R.
Wilner's "The Invisible Black Thread," in the special CLAJ
issue.   The title refers to an invisible black identity (repre-

sented by Tod and other "black" figures) which is pursuing
the narrator--unsuccessfully, since he is too busy in the
pursuit of a different identity.   This interplay marks the
book's comic and tragic levels but since the identities never
coalesce, the novel ultimately exhibits "an inability to digest the material of its own vision" (p. 243).   Wilner's
invisible black identity thesis seems to receive further support in Eugenia W. Collier's essay (special BlackW Ellison
issue, December, 1970) which analyzes Ellison's use of
dreams and other semiconscious states as conveyors of essential true aspects of Black life.

Despite Ellison's own statement of his attempt to explore the problems of black leadership in I. M. (see the 1961
interview by N. Samstag and Ted Cohen at the University of
Chicago), this aspect of the novel has only been dealt with
by M. K. Singleton (ArQ, Summer, 1966).   A less informative discussion of I. M. as symbolic history by Richard Kostelanetz covers some of the same territory, but without developing the theme beyond the obvious allusions to Booker
T. Washington (CR, 1967).

Literary protest and the incorporation of Ellison's
ideas on that subject into I. M. are analyzed by Charles T.
Ludington, Jr. in a "Protest and anti-Protest" symposium
(SHR, Winter, 1970).   Though no new viewpoints emerge
(the conclusion is that I. M. is "more than simply a Negro
protest novel, " p. 36), the essay is a useful summary of
arguments and attitudes.

Much useful material is added to Ellison studies by
two articles in the special CLAJ issue, which explore Ellison's use of myth and folklore.   Lawrence J. Clipper
analyzes the close correspondences between I. M. and the
motifs and situations of V. Propp's Morphology of the Folk-
tale, as well as Lord Raglan's morphology of the life of
mythic heroes.   Clipper feels that by using this strategy,
Ellison successfully diverts the white reader's attention away
from the perhaps disturbing negritude of the main character; by allowing him to respond on a subconscious and far
deeper human level to the centrality of a Negro in the novel,
Ellison thus greatly increases the reader's receptiveness.

Writing in the same issue, George E. Kent focuses
appreciatively on the uses of Afro-American folk and cultural
tradition in the novel, and on Ellison's repeated statements
on the importance of the subject. [6]  Finding that at many

points there is an elaborate interconnection between black
folk culture and Western symbols, Kent then expresses a
certain unease that such an interconnection was found neces-
sary.  "We would suppose that it is possible to sound the
depths of the universe by a fine excess in the examination of
Blackness," an examination of which Ellison has shown himself uniquely capable. [7]  Thus, the writers of these two essays on the uses of folk motifs express diametrically opposed assumptions and value judgments, which makes the
conjunction of their articles all the more interesting.

        Once again, as in the preceding period, R. W. B.
Lewis has opened up seminal areas of discussion in his consideration of Ellison within the context of his study of the
apocalyptic theme in its contemporary fictional permutations
(The Trials of the Word, 1965).  In examining the prevalence of a secularized apocalypse in current writing, Lewis
notes that contemporary treatment of this theme is unique
by virtue of its being suffused with a new and pervasive
sense of the absurd; catastrophe thus appears, as the relevant chapter indicates, in the guise of "Days of Wrath and
Laughter."  As an apocalyptic writer, Ellison exhibits the
same modern predilection, by converting the day of doom
(the Harlem riot) into a great saturnalia, a dies irae
risusque.  The riot is in the most literal sense "all hell
breaking loose" rather than a ritualized cathartic death and
rebirth process.  Ellison has elevated a political theme of
"making disaster serve the ends of conquest, into universal
apocalyptic significance" (p. 219).

        Suggestive as this analysis is, a closer examination
by Robert Alter (Commentary, June, 1966) of the concept of
apocalypse itself and of the oversimplifications into which
purely apocalyptic fiction may fall deepens the argument
further.  In this essay, the prophetic tradition--a tradition
requiring engagement with the threats and complexities of
history--is contrasted with the apocalyptic tradition, which
may simply lead one into an attitude of withdrawal from an
unbearable history.  The "Wrath and Laughter" stance,
Professor Lewis notes, may be socially less than desirable:

            To absolutize a lack of faith in man and history
            and project it into literature is, for an artist, an
            easy way out, an escape from the difficult respon-
            sibility of his calling.  Through a habit of nervous
            laughter over the world's going to pieces, we titil-
            late ourselves to the prospect, so that it may

become just a little more likely. Conversely, by carefully attending to the bewildering human particularities of our world, with the assumption that they must and can be coped with, we may make it somewhat more likely that we can grab hold of history before it goes skidding off to that awaited End. (p. 66)

Applied to I. M., these distinctions allow a direct perception of the book's salutary preoccupation with the particular, the complex and the threatening; quite properly, Professor Alter considers it "finally more serious" than most purely "apocalyptic" literature, and exempts it from sharing all the attributes of that class.

Doubtless due to the influence of the times, the theme of apocalypse has also generated premonitory shivers and localized interpretations, especially among white readers. Stephen B. Bennett and William W. Nichols conclude an article on violence in Afro-American fiction with their "appalling" discovery that

> the kind of apocalyptic rage commonly associated with contemporary black militants has been part of the imaginations of the best black writers in America for some time. (MFS, Summer, 1971, p. 228)

And Father John R. May's examination of "Images of Apocalypse in the Black Novel" (Renascence, Autumn, 1970) brings him to the insight that "we are indeed in the last days," a formulation which does not begin to do justice to the rich conceptions of the theme in the books he discusses.

Robert Alter's view on the necessity for responsible writing is shared by Nathan A. Scott from a slightly different vantage point, but one which similarly highlights I. M.'s serious preoccupations: at a time, he says, when many writers are committed "to the registration of the tremors of the self's experience of its own inwardness in an adverse world," Ellison's focus "is on the self, but on the self at that point of juncture where it encounters a significant social reality"[8] (UDQ, Summer, 1967, p. 223; this penetrating essay is further discussed in pp. 58-59 below).

For a black man, finding the self may involve, as Fanon has shown, a process of radical disalienation. In

her comparative analysis of Fanon and Ellison, Frances
Foster demonstrates that for Ellison even that process of
disalienation is social rather than purely individual, since
part of the process involves a reaffirmation of American
values and the American past (BlackAR, Winter, 1970).
Thus, from three different standpoints involving the concepts
of self, of the black self, and of the doomed world (apocalypse), I. M.'s integrity and inclusiveness clearly emerge,
refuting Edward Margolies' verdict that there is a certain
"thematic weakness" in the novel (Native Sons, 1968.  See
also David C. Howard's brief argument, taking direct issue
with Margolies, NConL, 1971).


Form, tone, character

     Most of the essays in this category reveal a contin-
uing tendency to apprehend I. M. mostly through the limited
process of relating it to traditional Western models.  A
danger in such an approach is the obscuring of the book's
diversity in the effort to impose upon it the purity of a
single form or attitude.  On the other hand, the variety of
models perceived to be functionally relating to the novel is
in itself a telling evidence of the book's rich transcendence
of the singular.

     The pattern of the Künstlerroman in I. M. is traced
by John Z. Bennett (XUS, March, 1966), while Richard
Pearce sees the novel as a parody of the related form of
the Bildungsroman (Stages of the Clown, 1970).  More
ancient models, such as the epic prototype are also drawn
upon.  Stewart Lillard (EJ, September, 1969) sees I. M.
as a successful attempt to produce "the great American
Negro epic."  His essay is particularly fruitful in its
references to several of Ellison's little-known early short
stories.  This whole area of Ellison's early fiction would
surely repay investigation, yet hardly any critic, with the
exception of the formidably erudite Ernest Kaiser, has taken
it up.  Very close to Lillard, though much more elaborated,
is Archie D. Sanders' discussion of I. M. as a novel in the
Odyssean mold (CLAJ, March, 1970); and Ronald G. Rollins
(Explicator, November, 1971) reads the Liberty Paints episode as an epic descent into hell, with Lucius Brockway as
the devil figure.  But Marcia R. Lieberman argues that the
analogy between Ulysses and the protagonist is a false one,
given the latter's naiveté, innocence, earnestness, and lack
of wiliness (CLAJ, September, 1971).  And, inasmuch as it

describes the birth of an anti-hero rather than of a traditional hero, William J. Schafer feels that the novel is only
"a fragment of an epic in form" (Critique, 1968).

While not dealing directly with the epic mold, Raney
Stanford's discussion of the trickster hero (JPC, Winter,
1967) is related to the Odyssean perspective.  He sees in
this ancient, morally ambivalent figure the very antithesis of
our conventional hero, returning to our fiction today as its
only resource for asserting vital values and freedom in a
society dehumanizing man.

A diametrically opposite analysis of form and character is offered by Nancy M. Tischler (ConL, Summer,
1969) who praises Ellison for attaining classic form in his
depiction of the Negro in the comic manner (Styron is said
to have attained the classic tragic manner in this area).
The classic (not classical) models to which Tischler has
reference are Candide and Gulliver's Travels.  Apart from
its interest as a reading at variance with the epic interpretations, Tischler's presentation highlights a rather common
fallacy whereby recognizable adherence of a work to traditional Western literary models constitutes a major criterion
of that work's value.  The underlying assumption is that
only these Western molds are suitable vehicles for "grand"
conceptions and universal meaning.  Cf., for example,
Stuart Miller's reasoning at the conclusion of his book,
The Picaresque Novel (1967), that a classification of I. M.
as an authentic picaresque novel confers additional value on
the work and "may have enlarged this novel's meaning.
Viewed one way, the book is simply a novel about the problems of Negroes.  But from another perspective, we see,
the book has wider appeal and wider meaning.  It is a
picaresque novel...." (p. 135).  Such examples of cultural
chauvinism may readily account for the insistence in some
quarters on the adoption of alternative, non-Western "classic" prototypes.  It may also explain the disappointment
of some black intellectuals that a writer of Ellison's calibre
chose to relate his work at so many crucial points to the
Western cultural heritage, rather than pioneering in an independent direction.  As Clifford Mason put it in the special
BlackW Ellison issue:

> The burden that Ellison's genius put on his man-
> hood (and what our racial needs required) was for
> him to have been a lion sui generis, not an ac-
> quiescer posing as a tiger.  Black literature

44                                        The Blinking Eye

deserved its own references, its own standards,
its own rules.. Not in an aberrant denial of anything that came from white American culture, valid
or otherwise, but as a conscious insistence on the
creating of an African American text that derived
its raison d'être from an African American truth
that exists in spite of the fact that it has never,
until very recently, had a really pervasive life in
the world of literature. (p. 21)

Tischler's thesis elicits a rebuttal from Thomas A. Vogler
on the grounds of faulty presentation--confusion of comic
genres, misrepresentation, limited vision, and oversimplification. Vogler does not, however, take issue with the basic
attitudes underlying the essay under consideration. See "An
Ellison Controversy," which also includes Tischler's rejoinder.

William J. Schafer in "Irony From Underground ..."
thinks a simple classification of I. M. as comic does not
reflect its complexity; for in fact, what he sees as the use
of satiric irony allows the novel to partake not only of the
Negro sense of comedy, but also of the tragicomic vision
of contemporary literature.

Related to discussions of the book's comic strain
is Richard Pearce's view of the protagonist as a clown
(Stages of the Clown, 1970). Including Ellison in a chapter with Grass and Beckett, he sees in these three writers
(in that order) a progressive affirmation of madness, in
repudiation of the Western ideal of rationality and progress.
The comedy lies in the reversals of reality, but the aim is
serious, striving always toward a more humanistic order.
Pearce points to analogies between these strategies and those
of the ancient Commedia dell'arte Harlequin--comic arch
destroyer of order without being a rebel.

As an extreme of the comic view, but here in its
brightest sense, we find Richard H. Rupp's reading of I. M.
as "a riotous feast of the self," "probably the major festive
novel of our period" (Celebration in Postwar American Fiction 1945-1967, 1970). Here every major incident in the
novel is interpreted as either a celebration or a chance of
it along the protagonist's progress toward manhood and
Negroness. The riot in particular is festive, celebrating
death and rebirth, and the killing of Ras functions as an
archetypal attempt to "introduce order and reality into riot
and illusion" (p. 162).

> Bracing peals of laughter echo on and on under
> the surface of I. M.  The whole is an elaborate
> musical and verbal joke, celebrating love, sacri-
> fice, and self-knowledge as our ultimate resources
> against the vicissitudes of life. (p. 164)

To qualify this rather one-dimensional view of the
book's comic tone and form, one would be well-advised to
read this essay in conjunction with R. W. B. Lewis' analysis
in Trials of the Word.  Lewis probes beneath the surface
manifestation of literary riotous feasts, to disclose their
mingled elements of "wrath and laughter" as well as their
intimate relationship to visions of ultimate doom--a far cry
from mere celebration for its own sake.

The stress on the comic in this period at least
signals a distinct change from the earlier tendency to highlight the book's pitiful/tragic aspects.  When vestiges of
this earlier approach occasionally surface, they sound
rather dated--Alfred Kazin's image of the best black voice
as "the gifted, unbearably frustrated man crying out for
life, for more and more access to life" (SR, October 2,
1971), or F. W. Dupee's insistence on "the generic loneliness of the systematically excluded and persecuted Negro"
(NYHT, September 26, 1965).  Nowadays, the book no longer
constitutes an outlet for white pity, and its tragic elements
are dealt with more broadly, as in Marcia L. Lieberman's
argument (CLAJ, September, 1971) that inasmuch as the
novel, like its predecessor, Candide, aims to show the
existence of evil, it is, comic elements notwithstanding, "a
tragic expression of life" (p. 77).  Less successful is Allen
Guttman's exploration of the literal and metaphoric uses of
nightmare (David Madden, American Dreams, American
Nightmares, 1970); the analysis here is not too revealing,
primarily because nightmare is most frequently made
synonymous with illusion, and this aspect of the novel as
a process of disillusionment is already quite familiar.

Antedating most of the discussions of form, yet far
more inclusive, is an essay by Therman B. O'Daniel, editor
of CLAJ, in that journal's June, 1967 issue.  Useful in its
summary of major critical approaches, this study is particularly profitable in its insistence that I. M. is "many
things in one," and that this diversity of formal and conceptual elements, arising out of Ellison's unique perspective on black life, constitutes the book's special excellence:

> It is then, this attitude, this philosophy of life,
> that enabled Ellison to portray in his novel, per-
> haps the best balanced and most complete and com-
> prehensive image of the American Negro that has
> yet been presented by any contemporary writer.
> Some realism, some pessimism, a considerable
> amount of disillusionment, some bitter irony and
> satire, and even some hate are all found in this
> unusual novel.  But since Ellison is definitely a
> romanticist and an optimist, some humor, some
> hope, and some love are also found in it. (p. 284)

Much of what O'Daniel interprets as salutary diversity
is read by Nick Aaron Ford as teasing ambivalence (BlackW,
December, 1970).  Citing several major examples in the
novel, as well as in Ellison's statements about it, Ford concludes that perhaps it is these aspects of the book which
account for its continued interest to readers.  One gets the
impression that writing of a bit more unequivocal nature
would not have been unwelcome to this scholar.

Lastly, one notes two essays which turn to non-
Western models, in this case, the blues.  Raymond H.
Olderman (WSCL, Summer, 1966) studies the use of the
blues as posture and intellectual perception; his essay has
much in common with that of Robert Bone which appeared
in the same year in TriQ, but which is far broader in scope.

## Structure

John Henrik Clarke's essay in the BlackW special
Ellison issue contains an interesting structural analysis of
the novel and it components; however, the writer's main
interest is not in technique, but in arguing with Ellison's
refusal to take an ideological stand.

The role of rhetoric as a structural device to "il-
luminate the conflict between opposing values and experiences" is closely examined by Lloyd W. Brown in the special CLAJ issue.

## Ellison Related to Other Writers

Some work has been done in this area, mostly in
relation to American writers.  Suggestions for many more

possible studies relating Ellison to major American and
European traditions are offered in Stewart Rodnon's "Ralph
Ellison's Invisible Man:   Six Tentative Approaches" (CLAJ,
March, 1969).

Three articles explore major nineteenth century American works which serve as ironic sources for I. M. :   Marvin
E. Mengeling notes (WWR, September, 1966) that Barbee's
sermon makes ironic use of many of the symbols in Whitman's "When Lilacs Last in the Dooryard Bloomd" (such as
the lilac, star, thrush, bells, funeral train).   William W.
Nichols, Phylon, Spring, 1970, analyzes the ironic use made
of Emerson's American Scholar and of his vision of the
American Dream.   Barbara Fass, CLAJ, March, 1971,
argues that insofar as Hawthorne's "My Kinsman Major
Molineux" has been allegorized as a fable of America's
emancipation from colonial bondage, it may serve as an
ironic source for I. M.   The rejection of paternalism, an
inherently American theme common to both books, trans-
lates with great ease into the experience of black Americans,
and there is further irony in the fact that in the literature
of colonial America may be found a paradigm of the black
struggle for identity.

On a strictly comparative level, Stewart Rodnon,
NALF, July, 1970, studies the close thematic and stylistic
correspondences between Huckleberry Finn and I. M., concluding on this basis that I. M. is, like its predecessor, a
central cultural document which represents as well the
height of black literary achievement.   Here is another
variant of the "praise by association" tendency already noted
earlier.

Moving into the twentieth century, Michael Allen
notes Ellison's use of Faulknerian rhetoric as a means of
rendering a language both "internal" and saturated with the
specific Southern cultural vision, also as a means of com-
peting with "a great white papa" of American letters (The
Black American Writer, ed. C. W. E. Bigsby, 1969).

Surprisingly little has been done in relating Ellison
to a black tradition of belles lettres (but see pp. 56-57
below).   Also, in view of his early personal association
with Richard Wright and his strong repudiation of him as
a literary influence (see "The World and the Jug" in S & A)
the absence of close comparative examination of their writings
is strange.   Hardly anyone in the fifties or sixties takes

advantage of the suggestive fact that I. M., Go Tell It On
the Mountain, and The Outsider appeared within a year of
each other (but see Steven Marcus' essay in 1953, Harold
Isaacs' in 1960, Irving Howe's in 1963 and the "Three
Negro Novelists:  Protest and Anti-Protest" symposium
described in SHR, 1970).  One reason might lie in the feeling that as one critic put it,

> their work [Wright's and Baldwin's] ... does not
> approach the artistic stature of Ellison's novel,
> and since Ellison considers himself an artist first
> and a Negro second, perhaps it is wiser to leave
> this avenue of examination unexplored here.
> (Stewart Rodnon, CLAJ, March, 1969, p. 255)

Another, hopefully more prevalent rationale for bypassing
such studies might be the desirability of avoiding the often
criticized parochial confrontation of one black writer with
another, as well as the fact that comparisons with Wright
inevitably run the danger of degenerating into the third
polemics involving Marxism and protest fiction.  But the
obvious similarities between Wright's 1944 novella, "The
Man Who Lived Underground, " and Ellison's Invisible Man
have elicited comment from a handful of critics.  William
Goede, MFS, Winter, 1969-70, concentrates on denying
Wright's influence on Ellison; he argues that in spite of surface similarities between the two works, Wright's novella
is not Ellison's source; it lacks significant development,
whereas Ellison's hero develops and changes; moreover,
Wright "evades the specifics of black history, " whereas
"Invisible Man by being specific, becomes also the symbolic history of America itself" (p. 491).  Similarly, in an
unpublished lecture before the Tennessee Philological Association, Elizabeth C. Phillips argues that I. M. in a sense
constitutes "a view of reality which forms an argument
with that of the earlier work, " in the treatment of horror,
in developing a point of view, and in its general outlook
on present and future.

Quite the opposite consideration is given to Wright
by some black intellectuals who use him as a pawn in the
battle for an aggressive, monolithic black aesthetic and
elevate him to high priest of black letters.  (See for example the results of the ND, January, 1968, literary poll
discussed pp. 27-28 above.)  As against William Goede,
we find Clifford Mason writing in the special BlackW issue
deploring Ellison's unacknowledged debt to Wright's novella.

To him Wright's characters are much more realistic than
the invisible protagonist, especially since they try to destroy
their invisibility, whereas the latter only tries to understand
its existence.  Even more aggressive is Mason's Life piece
earlier in the same year (May, 1970), significantly entitled
"Native Son Strikes Home."  Here again, contrast rather
than similarity is explored; Mason contends that Ellison has
been elevated at the expense of Wright, but that it is Wright's
hero and not Ellison's who represents the real black experience, offering a solution to our problems as well as a prophetically realized model of the alternative to non-change.

Suggestive, rather than fully developed, is Robert E.
Fleming's essay on contemporary themes in James Weldon
Johnson's Autobiography of an Ex-Colored Man, and his
illustrations of this from the text of I. M., among several
other contemporary Negro novels (NALF, Winter, 1970).
The major themes are: namelessness, racial self-hatred,
the black mother's ambiguous role, and the characterization
of the white patron/white liberal.  Ellison is used in connection with the first and second, but could easily be used
in greater depth for these as well as for the remaining two
categories.

Finally, a comparison between I. M. and Fanon's
Black Skin, White Masks, the original French edition of
which also appeared in 1952, is undertaken by Frances
Foster, with most of the emphasis given, however, to Fanon
(BlackAR, Winter, 1970).  Nonetheless, the essay opens up
interesting avenues by comparing the very similar patterns
found in both books in the process of reaching self-awareness, though the resulting path to disalienation assumes ultimately different forms.

This, up to the end of 1971, is the sum total of published critical investigation of Ellison in the context of Afro-
American literary themes or motifs.  Much remains to be
done in this area, looking both backward and forward: for
example, there is the black Brotherhood in Griggs's Imperi-
um in Imperio;  the black versus the white consciousness
in Webb's The Garies and their Friends; the use of irony
in Chesnutt; the depiction of ambitious, unscrupulous blacks
in Hurston's Their Eyes Were Watching God, or Redding's
No Day of Triumph; and the uncanny similarity between the
black college in I. M. and in Larsen's Passing.  One could
check out the influence of Ellison on the work of some
younger writers such as William Melvin Kelley, Ernest
Gaines or Ishmael Reed.

Not much work has been done either in close study
of Ellison's modern European antecedents, though his in-
debtedness to Dostoevski is by now a critical platitude.
Several suggestions are made by Stewart Rodnon (CLAJ,
March, 1969), and a comparison with Candide in character,
narrative structure, point of view, and moral intention is
offered by Marcia Lieberman (CLAJ, September, 1971).
Curiously enough, scholars have overlooked André Malraux'
La Condition Humaine as an obvious major source for I. M. ,
not to mention the immediate antecedent of H. G. Wells's
novel of the same title.


## Essays Dealing with General Analysis

Robert Bone's widely reprinted 1966 essay in TriQ
remains among the most instructive studies of this general
kind.   Professor Bone makes a detailed application of S & A
to I. M. ; analyzes the jazz and blues elements as they trans-
late into conceptual and technical idiom; discusses Ellison's
literary heritage stressing the picaresque and the transcen-
dental traditions; and demonstrates the felicitous intermesh-
ing of all these in conveying the experience, as well as the
central values of American civilization.   Discussing another
major problem--the Ellison-Howe debate of 1963-64--he
suggests some useful distinctions between politics and art:
politics deal with remediable evil, art with the irremediable
(hence, with the tragic human dimension).   To use the
artistic imagination is to attend to both of those aspects,
as Ellison has done, since the black condition, like any
other, partakes of both; hence the area of remediable evil
(politics) cannot alone be made the touchstone of one's
humanity. [9]   Herein is the nub of the disagreement still
swirling around Ellison.   At opposite poles from Bone's
advocacy of creative independence, Ernest Kaiser most ably
defends the case for more utilitarian uses of the imagination.
In his long bibliographic essay in the special BlackW Ellison issue he berates Ellison for allegedly treating black
suffering as a metaphysical, hence irremediable, part of
the human condition, and thus advocating endurance at the
expense of resistance.   For Bone, Ellison's pluralistic,
non-ideological perspective is salutary, forging links to
heal the nation's shattered psyche; Kaiser attacks this very
posture as dehumanized and psychologically sick artistic
detachment.   Thus considerations of Ellison continue to
bring into question basic assumptions about the function of
art in general.

Analyzing I. M. in the same issue of BlackW, Clifford
Mason tempers praise for its technical mastery and sheer
literary achievement with a lengthy critique of the protagonist's confusion and passivity; he objects to Ellison's "ampli-
tude of literary references, " his efforts to establish universality and his "mainstream mentality, " and accuses him
of evading his responsibility as a black artist. [10]  The same
number of BlackW, however, finds Larry Neal striking a
difficult equilibrium between the positions of the Bone and
Kaiser camps.  Seriously attempting an assessment of his
own involvement with Ellison's art and ideas and their impact on his life, he develops insights which owe their per-
suasiveness to personal engagement rather than to rhetoric.
The main thrust of his argument (see "Special Ellison issues ..." p. 55 below), is that Ellison's writing at-
tests to his being a committed cultural nationalist; that I. M.
is permeated with a black aesthetic and with a deep understanding of the process by which black values are formed,
and that, in fact, Ellison has successfully transmuted politics into art.

On a less polemical level, Edward M. Griffin's essay
(TCL, October, 1969), is helpful in its comprehensive re-
capitulation of techniques in I. M.  He also proposes an
original view of the book's unifying theme, namely the hero's
progress from a state wherein he perceives the world as
fixed and solid, to a final apprehension of its unsettling
fluidity.

Taking as his point of departure the critical problems
faced by the reader of I. M., Thomas A. Vogler (IR, Spring,
1970), clarifies them in his own exposition of the novel
which is both broad and detailed.  He also offers interesting
speculations on the probable conceptual difficulties involved in
the writing of Ellison's long-delayed second novel: as a
sequel to I. M. it needs to be a redemptive fable, which
poses self-evident problems.

Reflecting I. M. 's economic and scholarly boom is the
publication by 1971 of at least two collections of criticism:
John M. Reilly's in the Twentieth Century Interpretations
Series (1970), and Ronald Gottesman's in the Charles Merrill Studies series (1971).  The former's 1970 date of publication precluded inclusion of important material from either
the CLAJ or the BlackW special Ellison issues of that same
year.  Despite its later appearance, Gottesman's volume
also lacks these materials, and as far as one can see,

reprints no black-authored essays at all.  It also suffers
by comparison with Reilly's work in its total lack of scholarly apparatus, as well as in the very small number of
critical selections, two of which (Robert Bone's essay on
the uses of the imagination and Floyd Horowitz on Brer
Rabbit) duplicate Reilly's.

A study guide for students is also available, edited
by Elizabeth C. Phillips for Monarch (1971).  This work
also lacks material from the special issues, but the bibliography points the student to other valuable black sources.
Since it is intended for use in literature courses, its approach to the novel leans heavily on structural and symbolic analysis.

## Special Ellison Issues of CLAJ and BlackW

These special numbers of black-edited journals appear in the same year, March and December, 1970, respectively, and offer illuminating contrasts; for while both
journals consider Ellison as a major writer, they share
little else in philosophy and content, as a brief consideration of their differences will show.

The essays in CLAJ are more academically oriented
than those in BlackW,  but the latter provides a bibliography
of primary and secondary materials, a task not undertaken
by CLAJ.  However, no special research seems to have
gone into this project, and the results are rather perfunc-
tory--the primary list seems to ignore the existence of
R. S. Lillard's bibliography, and the secondary list consists of the few well-known items already available elsewhere.  CLAJ's contributors are multiracial, whereas
BlackW uses a single white contribution jimcrowed in the
back of the issue away from the rest of the Ellison material.  And whereas all CLAJ essays are original contributions of high quality, BlackW chose to represent white
scholarship by reprinting a rather superficial 1966 "portrait"
interview of Ellison done by John Corry, significantly captioned here "A White View of Ralph Ellison."  Clearly, the
BlackW strategy here is polemic:  the choice of an old and
fairly banal piece, of an interview rather than a critical
analysis, conveniently serve to downgrade the seriousness
of white criticism and to illustrate a supposed gap between
white "cultism" of Ellison and the concerns of any serious
black reader.  A more subtle reason for the choice of Corry

might be his account of Ellison's refusal to sign an anti-
Vietnam petition circulated at the White House Festival on
the Arts, since he felt it to be "ir bad taste when we were
guests of the President." Perhaps black readers were
meant to reach the same conclusion as that expressed elsewhere by J. Hagopian that Ellison was exploiting "a limited
literary achievement by muzzling [himself] politically in the
name of good taste and manners in return for favors from
the government and the conservative establishment" ("Mau-
mauing ... ", p. 144). This kind of judgment by innuendo,
reflects the issue's focus on the expression of attitudes toward Ellison, and is consistent with BlackW's past practice
(see pp. 26-27 above). CLAJ, on the other hand, attempts
nothing more than to convey the range of current scholarly
appraisals of Ellison's work.

      As already noted, the articles in CLAJ are almost
without exception of impeccably high standards. Consider-
ing the profusion of material already available on Ellison,
it comes as a pleasant surprise that so many of the essays
in this issue should add materially to an understanding of
the novel, and on levels far removed from the abstract
myth-mongering commonly associated with academic criticism. On the other hand, the unevenness of the BlackW
material lends that issue a far more dramatic quality.
Contributions here range from a two-page personal appeal
to Ellison by novelist John A. Williams, to an incredibly
learned 23-page discussion of Ellison's work and critics
by Ernest Kaiser of the Schomburg Library. But whereas
CLAJ offers variety by way of its diverse critical approaches,
much of the material in BlackW, in spite of varied formulation and intensity, simply amounts to a dramatization of the
differences between Ellison and his black critics on questions
of artistic integrity and of "black" reality. Judging by
these pieces, the "unholy alliance" of Negro artist and
Negro scholar in racial chauvinism, of which Theodore Gross
complained in 1968 ("Our Mutual Estate: the Literature of
the American Negro," AR, 28, no. 3, Fall, 1968, 293-303),
certainly seems to have dissolved in the case of Ellison.

      Most of the essays in these issues have already been
discussed in their appropriate contexts. Only the contributions of Ernest Kaiser and Larry Neal in BlackW will be
taken up here, since in their contrary assumptions and their
respective merits they constitute a highlight of the issue.

      Ernest Kaiser's essay well justifies its comprehensive

title ("A Critical Look at Ellison's Fiction and at Social and
Literary Criticism by and about the Author"). Tracing
Ellison's writing career, he argues that it shows great regression after 1943. Prior to that, Ellison's association
with New Masses showed true social concern, but this, his
"healthiest and best" period is replaced by esoteric concerns with culture, folklore, psychology, and pernicious
assimilation of New Criticism doctrines, defined here in
their extreme as "art for art's sake." The post-1943 short
stories, as well as I. M., take no account of black reality,
anti-Communism and the total artificiality of contrived
myths and symbols having replaced true concern with people. No change is evident in the essays and published excerpts from the second novel; all still center on abstrac-
tions ("birds, flight and castration symbolism," p. 85)
and truisms, and all lack compassion for those who are
destroyed by American conditions.

There follows a discussion of critical reactions to
Ellison, with approval for the early left-oriented black
criticism, and a regretful shake of the head for more recent black academic critics who seem "mesmerized" by
white encomiums (the special CLAJ issue is cited here);
as for white critics, they have turned Ellison into a fad
and have demonstrated their usual presumption in authenti-
cating his vision of black life despite their own ignorance
of it. (Here, Kaiser chooses to ignore the growing number
of black critics who have also endorsed the authenticity of
Ellison's depiction of "the real" black experience.)

Representing as he does the political, versus what
Robert Bone has called the tragic sensibility, Kaiser would
use art as a weapon for concrete social change. Missing
that dimension in Ellison, he feels the latter is wrongly
stressing endurance rather than resistance, individual response rather than collective effort to bring about change.
"Doesn't he want real black heroes and heroines?" Kaiser
asks. From this perspective Ellison's art appears detached,
exploitative of suffering since he offers no concrete remedy
to it, and hence dehumanized.

One may find the Marxist perspective repugnant, and
yet sympathize somewhat with Kaiser's argument, as when
one reads a distinguished white American's pronouncement
that "basically the issue isn't to 'solve' the 'race problem'
... You don't solve it, you just experience it. Appreciate
it." (Robert Penn Warren, Paris Review, 16, Spring-

Summer, 1957, 136). Even with allowances for a deeper
meaning, such a statement brings a realization of the pitfalls involved in too detached a view of social problems.
One can welcome the kind of criticism Mr. Kaiser so
cogently represents, as a healthy reminder of the very concrete dimensions of art which are too often ignored by more
abstract intellectualizing.

One one level Larry Neal's essay may almost be
read as a rebuttal to Kaiser and his school of socially
oriented criticism. Though Neal also rejects an exclusively
aesthetic evaluation of any literary work, he cautions
against the dangers of programmed art, and feels that most
attacks on Ellison are invalidated by virtue of their over-
simplified Neo-Marxian assertions. His reading of Ellison's
early work reveals a consistent rejection of sectarian
Marxism and a thrust toward Negro folk culture as a real
source of strength. Most of Neal's essay explores Ellison's
positive and vital contribution to black cultural nationalism;
the latter's creative orientation as distinct from his political
activism is a prime factor in his expression and celebration
of black traditions and of the values they shape. On the
controversial question of Ellison's cultural pluralism, Neal
lucidly suggests that awareness of the best works ever
written does not turn one white; and while he disagrees with
limiting one's cultural enquiry to Europe and America, he
is equally reluctant to recommend exclusive attention to
Africa and African subjects. In sum, in what constitutes a
dramatic reversal of his own earlier views, [11] Neal acknowl-
edges a personal and artistic debt to Ellison and pleads for
creative freedom, even in periods of political contest. It
is of course too early to tell, but perhaps Neal's serious
reappraisal of Ellison is destined to mark the beginning of
a new era in which the orthodoxies of the "black aesthetic"
will be broadened in the interest of black unity rather than
divisiveness.


Discussions Within Broader Contexts

As the heading of this section indicates, the material
covered here consists of specialized studies wherein Ellison,
though not a primary subject, receives more than passing
attention. Some of the more seminal findings in this category have already been discussed earlier.

The two major contexts within which Ellison finds

consideration to date, are the area of African and Afro-
American literature, and that of contemporary American
fiction.


1.   African-American Literature

     Ellison and others are examined in Nancy Tischler's
Black Masks:   Negro Characters in Modern Southern Fiction
(1969).   Several other studies draw partly upon Ellison in
the attempt to pinpoint some distinctive traits of an Afro-
American literary tradition:   Theodore L. Gross (Phylon,
Spring, 1971) sees the best of Afro-American writing as
characterized by a pervasive idealism coexisting with violence, and expressed by means of religious fervor, a sense
of history, a Romantic point of view and a deep concern
with the possibilities of language.   Consideration of Ellison
forms the backbone of this essay.   (The problems of idealism versus authority as they pertain to all American literature are taken up more fully in Gross's 1971 book, The
Heroic Ideal in American Literature.)   Stephen B. Bennett
and William W. Nichols (MFS, Summer, 1971) isolate as
a distinctive trait of twentieth century Afro-American fiction a preoccupation with violence as a creative possibility;
in their evident concern with the sociological implications of
this finding, the authors overlook the prevalence of violence
in most contemporary fiction.   Related to this is an earlier
essay by Father John R. May, S.J. (Renascence, Autumn,
1970), emphasizing the strong impact of the apocalyptic
tradition in the writing of twentieth century Afro-Americans,
and studying the treatment of this theme in Native Son, I.M.,
Go Tell It on the Mountain, and System of Dante's Hell
(see pp. 40-41 above for a discussion of the apocalyptic
tradition).   Here, too, the threat of violence seems to be
uppermost in the writer's mind.

     Raman K. Singh (ColQ, Summer, 1971) offers an
ambitious and comprehensive account of what he considers
two specifically Afro-American fictional traits:

     a) distinctive treatment of the American identity
quest theme; whereas the white American quest ends in a
variety of failures, the Afro-American quest ends in the
successful discovery of identity.   (Using different works--
though Native Son and I.M. are common to both studies--
John O'Brien, SBL, Autumn, 1971, reaches a contrary conclusion:   he sees the black hero as always in process of

becoming, and always stranded somewhere on the road to discovery, with the quest left incomplete. )

b) the concept of soul with its double-edged function as rejection of the machine culture of Western society and recognition that the black life-style may serve to reunite the head and heart of the West.  I. M. serves, among other works, to illustrate both of these aspects of soul.  Lloyd W. Brown may be hovering around the idea of "soul" in his detailed analysis of the symbolic use of names in much Afro-American literature, including I. M. (SBL, September, 1970).

In a more documentary approach, a posthumously published essay by William T. Fontaine (AForum, Spring-Summer, 1968), analyzes works of Afro-American fiction from Dunbar to Ellison, in order to provide an introduction to Negro cultural history and to demonstrate the importance of the concept of freedom in black thinking.  I. M., he suggests, prefigures what is "brilliantly realized in Martin Luther King:  the idea of a leadership, founded in action, nonviolent, without fear of death, concerned for the needs of white men as well as black" (p. 96).  Also in a political context, Michael Furay cites Ellison's writings in support of his contention that Negritude is a much attenuated concept for American Negroes (NR, July 2, 1966).  The representative quality here attributed to Ellison seems ridiculously illusory from the vantage point of 1973.

## 2.   American Literary Tradition

Within the context of modern absurdist fiction, Ellison combines a sense of the world's irrationality with a belief "in the fully lyric and expressive voice of visionary American fiction" (A. Kazin, MR, Spring, 1971).  Modern fiction is also concerned with the ironic nature of the alternatives open to man in a world where choice is itself absurd.  Ellison's I. M. coherently articulates these problems --"it posits the realm of the ironic alternatives in the contemporary novel:  conformity, destruction, or withdrawal" (Alvin Greenberg, in Madden's American Dreams ..., 1970, p. 180).

Ellison also appears in Ihab Hassan's study of "the Novel of Outrage" (ASch, Spring, 1965), as a powerful voice of postwar fiction at the stage where "outrage is

mediated by a residual faith in man's will ... dignity or
mind" (p. 246).

Examining the American novel as it develops an
"activist" mode as opposed to the Kafkan victim pattern,
Helen Weinberg (The New Novel in America, 1970) finds
I. M. partaking of both modes.

Of interest are three studies drawing upon a longer
historical perspective than the contemporary. The Heroic
Ideal in American Literature (1971) is studied by Theodore
L. Gross as a conflict between idealism and authority.
Within this framework, Negro writing emerges as the act
of creating literary heroes in challenge to American authority and its antagonism to Negro manhood; Ellison's work
(some short stories are discussed), standing in dialectical
relationship to Wright's and Baldwin's, is in a sense "a
satire on the myth of self-reliance, self-improvement, and
the heroic ideal" (p. 162), but with the idealism always
superimposed at the end, and increasingly affirmed in S & A.
Even without Gross's description of Ellison as "the Emerson
of American Negro writing, " we see him placed squarely in
the midst of central American and Afro-American values.
(See Gross's 1969 Phylon article which develops the idealism
of Negro literature more fully. )

The abiding influence of Puritanism and its secular
derivatives are discussed by James D. Boulger (Thought,
Autumn, 1969). Residual patterns of Election/Reprobation,
search for Vocation and related trials, and Glorification--
"the final sense of the self, and the meaning of the hero's
journey to his end for himself and for others" (p. 420)--
are pointed out in Last Hurrah, By Love Possessed, I. M.,
and Herzog, bearing witness to the imprint of those ideas
upon the American mind even in the case of Catholic, Black,
and Jewish writers. I. M. is judged to be the most consistent of the four novels examined in its allegorical use of the
pattern, as well as being "the most artistically successful
and significant" (p. 432).

Finally, in a provocative, closely argued essay
drawing upon yet another deep-rooted American theme--
that of the "wounded Adam"--Nathan A. Scott Jr. (UDQ,
Summer, 1967), asserts that this theme is most cogently
expressed by black American writers; hence it is they who
are found to be at the heart of the American cultural experience and imagination. Indeed, in this context of "the Amer-

ican as Adam, hectored and wounded by the world, " Negro
writers illustrate both the myth and its pitfalls, i. e. , the
fascination with evil.   In Ellison alone is there a control of
the myth:   he has "kept his Adam to a course that avoids
at once the Scylla of rampant nihilism [Wright] and the
Charybdis of inordinate self-pity [Baldwin]"; hence his work
constitutes "a triumph of art and of moral imagination"
(p. 34).   His hero is not only wounded, but well on his
way to healing maturity.   The value of such a study, like
that of Albert Murray's The Omni Americans (1970) and of
Ellison's own S & A, is that they nudge one toward appre-
hending the black experience as a central and significant
projection of the total' American experience, rather than as
a negligible catalogue of a minority's "plight and blight. "

## Notes

1.   Four years later, however, in Waiting for the End,
      Fiedler is much less enthusiastic about the novel's
      ability to convey truth, criticizing it as looking back-
      ward, being "disconcertingly reminiscent of Kafka's
      K, " and seeming like "a secondhand version of the
      black man in America" (p. 107).

2.   Irving Howe is less ready than Lewis to be convinced
      of the positive contribution of modern fiction.   Prais-
      ing I. M. along with other best efforts of the period,
      he contends that "all these novels merit admiration
      for defending the uniqueness of man's life, but ...
      [their] proclamation of personal identity ... tends ...
      to be more a product of the will than of the imagina-
      tion. "  See "Mass Society and Post Modern Fiction, "
      Partisan Review, 26, no. 3 (Summer, 1959), 420-
      436.

3.   Two shorthand translations of this might be subsumed
      in the still fashionable view of I. M. as a good novel
      because it is "a novel about a Negro ... but ... not
      really a Negro novel, " e. g. , R. Lehan, CEJ (1965),
      or the mod reading of Afro-American writing as
      representing a symbolic "black mask of humanity"
      and "image of man's fate, " S. L. Gross and J. E.
      Hardy, eds. , Images of the Negro in American Lit-
      erature, 1960, pp. 25-26.

4.   Jay B. Hubbell, Who Are the Major American Writers?

Durham, N.C., Duke University Press, 1972, pp. 282-283.

5. Baldwin's sharp insight is expressed in a passing comment in the "Autobiographical Notes" to Notes of a Native Son (1955): "Mr. Ellison, by the way, is the first Negro novelist I have ever read to utilize in language, and brilliantly, some of the ambiguity and irony of Negro life."

6. Cf. also his earlier essay "Ethnic Impact in American Literature: Reflections on a Course," CLAJ, 11, no. 1 (September, 1967), 24-37, where a similar point about Ellison is made.

7. But cf. the contrary thesis in Gerald W. Haslam's essay--#200.

8. See in this connection R.W.B. Lewis' "Recent Fiction: Picaro and Pilgrim."

9. Cf. also the almost identical argument in Seymour L. Gross and John E. Hardy, eds., Images of the Negro in American Literature. Chicago, University of Chicago Press, 1966, p. 19.
   Generally speaking, the growing dissatisfaction with Negro protest literature reflected the wider disillusionment with all forms of social hopefulness.... Naturally, a critical disposition that oriented itself toward 'the tragic vision' (the inevitable betrayal at the heart of things) would not find much viability in any literary program based on the assumption that life's evils are sociologically reversible.

10. We are a long way from Blyden Jackson's prescription for "A Golden Mean For the Negro Novel," which he applauds recent black novelists of his day, Ellison among them, for illustrating (CLAJ, September, 1959). The essay's conclusion is here quoted in full, for purposes of comparison with the standards of today's "black aesthetic."
    But, happily, the most perceptive of the Negro novelists within our generation have interpreted well their most pressing duty and their brightest opportunity. That duty and that opportunity are to trace the growing assimilation of the Negro to

the American middle class, to make constantly
more known the process by which the Negro ...
is consolidating his position, in fact and in symbol, between the never-never Cytherea of the
Clotel complex, on the one hand, and the roman-
ticizing of a black proletariat, on the other.
This is a middleground which is a golden mean
for the Negro novel in its role as protestant
against the exclusion of the Negro from the norms
of American life.

11. Cf. Neal's comments on I. M. in his afterword to
    Black Fire (1968):
      The things that concerned Ellison are interesting
      to read, but contemporary black youth feels an-
      other force in the world today.  We know who we
      are, and we are not invisible,  at least not to each
      other.  [Neal's emphasis]  We are not Kafkaesque
      creatures stumbling through a white light of con-
      fusion and absurdity.  The light is black (now,
      get that!) as are most of the meaningful tendencies
      in the world. (p. 652)

FRANCE - ESSAYS

# INTRODUCTION

The reception of Ellison in France is an anomalous mixture of neglect and spotty appreciation: the first French version of I. M. published in 1954 (Au delà du regard, tr. Michel Chrestien, Paris: Editions Denoël) is met by total indifference, attracting one lone review before passing into oblivion. No other translation is made available to the French reader until 1969, fifteen years later, nor is there any evidence that Ellison spent extensive time in France. Yet despite this limited exposure, the French government in 1968 chooses to honor Ellison by conferring upon him the prestigious Order of Chevalier des Arts et des Lettres.[1] Regrettably, though, this award contributes nothing toward building up Ellison's reputation and enlarging his French readership, for the extraordinary reason that it remains unpublicized; not a single one of the numerous French scholars who have dealt with Ellison's work seems aware of their government's initiative in honoring this author.

In 1969, Bernard Grasset publishers brought out a new and superior translation of I. M. by Robert and Magali Merle, entitled Homme invisible, pour qui chantes-tu? (Hereafter, H. I.) This time around, the novel is widely reviewed in some of the major papers and journals; though sociologically oriented, most of the reviews are of a high calibre and take advantage of their more advanced historical perspective to make some telling points. Several are, indeed, openly self-gratulatory in the consciousness of having advanced beyond the early American myopia toward the book. Nonetheless, this flurry of publicity does not appear to have generated a more permanent interest in Ellison, who to date remains the subject of respectful but detached interest.

Perhaps one explanation for this attitude lies in the nature of French preconceptions about American as well as black writing. With respect to the former, the French have come only fairly late, and in some cases very tentatively,

to a recognition of its existence as a distinct branch of world literature, [2] and their general conception of its characteristics is
remarkably stereotyped: what they identify as "le style américain" is writing of a neo-primitive, exotic, violent and anti-in-
tellectual nature. [3] While readers of the 1950's might have found
Au delà du regard too overpowering an example of a mode they
had temporarily wearied of, the book may ironically have come
to seem too urbane to readers of the 1960's, mesmerized by the
flamboyant literary mayhem committed upon them by younger
black writers.

      To the stereotypes about American literature, one must
add the low regard or rather, non-recognition of black American literature as a factor influencing the academic reaction to
Ellison. While Wright, Himes and Hughes are familiar to the
French reader, the first indeed being considered as the cultural
spokesman for his race, only jazz and poetry are recognized
and respected as distinct Afro-American cultural products. [4]
When these assessments forcibly readjust themselves in the
1960's, they do so in a context of political rather than cultural
changes. Reflecting the seemingly ubiquitous propensity for focusing only on one black writer at a time, the French then cata-
pult LeRoi Jones directly into the niche left vacant by Richard
Wright's death in 1960. His writings are translated and eagerly
read, his pronouncements on various matters are uncritically
repeated, and, worse, he is made the point of access to discussions of other black writers, especially Ellison. The latter is
indeed the subject of some very penetrating studies; but reference materials about him are scarce and inadequate, and none
of his work except for I. M. has been translated. The overall
treatment of him leaves the distinct impression that he is considered passé--pending such time as French readers' appetite
for the sensational shall be satiated and replaced by a genuine
desire to take the Afro-American experience seriously.

## I.  BIOGRAPHICAL INFORMATION

      French reference books (discussed in III below) provide
only minimal information on Ellison's life and career, omitting
even the fact of the official French distinction bestowed upon
him. Such scarce interview material as is available consists of
reprints of American interviews, or of reported meetings with
Ellison in New York.

      One remarkably early source documenting some of Elli-

son's major thinking is the journal Preuves, which in 1958 que-
ried what it considered as the leading black intellectuals of all
nationalities on the subject of Black Culture. Ralph Ellison is
included alongside such notables as Léopold Sedar Senghor and
Richard Wright. His replies to Preuves' questions are the earliest available French exposition of his ideas on the specificity of
a Black American culture, which can only be understood as an
active interrelationship of both its major terms.

Ten years later, in 1968, the editors of the semi-official
I&D, 5 in a curiously belated effort to remedy what they consider
to be a lack of information about Ellison in France, reprint in
their March 15 issue excerpts from 1965 interviews of Ellison
by three young black writers in New York. (The original interview appeared in the 1967 Harper's Magazine under the title "A
Very Stern Discipline.") In its very abbreviated French version,
this interview does not fill an appreciable gap, for much of its
content may be found in Preuves and, more recently, in Pierre
Dommergues' 1967 study, Les U. S. A. à la recherche de leur
identité (see III below).

Readers of the Swiss Journal de Genève are offered in its
July, 1970 literary supplement translated excerpts from an e-
qually old interview by Robert Penn Warren in Who Speaks for
the Negro? (1965). As for direct interviews of Ellison by French
critics, only two have so far turned up, and both took place in
New York rather than in France. (Pierre Dommergues also interviewed Ellison, directly or by correspondence; but since he
only provides very short excerpts, interspersed with quotes from
S & A and other writings, one lacks a sense of the personal encounter, if such it was.) The first interview by Naim Kattan,
LanM (May-June, 1966), explores mostly Ellison's attitude toward the black liberation movement. The second, by Anne Thinesse, FL, August 11-17, 1969, appears at the time of H. I. 's publication. It is a most peculiar piece of writing: entitled "Ralph
Ellison est-il autre chose qu'un Oncle Tom qui a reussi?"6 it
seems to have lifted most of its contents from John Corry's 1966
interview of Ellison ("An American Novelist Who Sometimes
Teaches," NYT Book Review, November 20), but with the materials arranged so as to affirm the title's rhetorical question and
Uncle Tom allegation. In all fairness to French critics, Thinesse's methods appear to be totally non-representative.

Clearly much work remains to be done in exposing Ellison's person and ideas to the French public.

## II.  BIBLIOGRAPHIES

No bibliography of primary or secondary materials is
available in any of the French sources consulted.  Some French
criticism may be found through the excellent bibliographic pam-
phlet compiled by Christiane Laude, chief librarian of the Benjamin Franklin Documentation Center, Services Américains d'Information et de Relations Culturelles, entitled Panorama critique
du roman américain contemporain (1967).  But since Laude's
work is intended to acquaint the French reader with American
background materials on the contemporary American novel, the
bulk of her list consists of general books on the subject which
are written in English; periodical articles are entirely omitted.
In the absence of reliable French indices comparable to the an-
nual MLA bibliography of literature, the student must resort to
luck and ingenuity in unearthing critical material on Ellison and
the risk of omissions is consequently far greater.

## III.   GENERAL ESTIMATES - REFERENCE WORKS
## AND LITERARY HANDBOOKS

The French reader turning to major reference
sources in search of information on Ellison is apt to be
disappointed.  No entry appears in the Grand Larousse
(1961), or in the three prestigious reference works by
Laffont-Bompiani, Dictionnaire biographique des auteurs
(1956, 2nd ed., 1964), Dictionnaire des personnages (1960),
and Dictionnaire des lettres (1961).  Ellison is (although
unlisted in the index) included in Philippe Van Tieghem,
Dictionnaire des littératures, I (1968); the whole entry,
however, includes only two dates--of Ellison's birth, and
of the publication of I. M.  One is struck in general by the
paucity of factual apparatus in most French sources.

Two works which anthologize Ellison and comment
on him are Leonard Sainville's Anthologie de la littérature
négro-africaine (1963), and Michel Fabre's Les Noirs
américaines (1968).  Neither author seems aware of the
existence of Au delà du regard.  Sainville's point of view
combines Marxism and negritude; he conceives of his book
as a weapon in the universal black liberation struggle, dis-
claims any attention to stodgy scholarship and has read
nothing of Ellison's except I. M.  Though Ellison and black
Americans who share Sainville's views have long mutually

deplored each other, Sainville not only includes Ellison in
his collection but also praises him in the highest terms as
"un militant politique et antiraciste." Apart from the collection's obvious bias, it is short on facts and accuracy:
the five-page summary of I. M. is often erroneous, and biographical data are said to have been "impossible to obtain."
Thus the inclusion of Ellison here is mostly of historical
interest.

The second anthology, Michel Fabre's Les Noirs
américains, differs from Sainville in aim and content: its
two major divisions offer a historical-sociological survey of
black life in America from 1620 to the Black Power Revolution, and an anthology of Afro-American writing inclusive of
essays, documents and folk literature. To the traditional
snippet from I. M. by which Ellison is commonly represented,
Fabre also adds a translation of an essay on the blues.
The book has a useful primary bibliography of Afro-American writings with a helpful list of translations. I. M. is
marked as among the "livres essentiels" and though Fabre
omits the 1954 translation, he alerts his readers to the
forthcoming translation by Grasset; S & A is also listed.
(Fabre has since collaborated on a primary Ellison bibliography for 1937-1971, published in an Afro-American
journal. See U. S. bibliography, section II).

Fabre's book is a much needed addition to knowledge
of Afro-American culture in a historical and sociological
perspective. It cannot, however, substitute for a work of
thorough literary criticism, though it does provide some of
the tools needed for such a study.

Pierre Brodin's Présences contemporaines: écrivains
américains d'aujourd'hui des années 50 (1964), dealing with
authors born after 1914, is ambiguous in its treatment of
Ellison: on the one hand he isolates him as a black author,
comparing him only with Wright and Baldwin, and noting
that I. M. is considered the most important novel ever written about "the black problem." On the other hand, his discussion of the novel completely eliminates considerations of
race or racism, dealing with it as though it took place in
a vacuum of abstract universal notions. 7 The terms in
which he praises the novel are particularly interesting, for
to the conventional citing of vividness, humor, construction
and so on, he adds applause for its power in typically
French terms: the book, he says, "gives the reader the
impression of having been picked up by a bulldozer. "8

Brodin lists only one essay and I. M. as a primary
bibliography, and provides no secondary criticism.   An ap-
pendix reprints authors' responses to Brodin's queries about
their reading, among them a letter from Ellison citing his
favorite French authors.

In his 1969 sequel which updates many of the authors
discussed in 1964 (Ecrivains américains d'aujourd'hui des
années 60), Brodin omits Ellison entirely, on the grounds
that he has written nothing since I. M. --a regrettable display
of ignorance, in light of S & A and other evidence of Ellison's writing activity.   Brodin also, in the same place,
dismisses Ellison as an integrationist, thus clearly reflecting the intrusion of politics into literary appreciation.

The treatment of Ellison in two handbooks from the
popular series "Que Sais-Je?" ranges from the misleading
to the nonexistent.   Pierre Dommergues' Les écrivains
américains d'aujourd'hui (1965) excises a very specific
dimension of I. M. in his assertion that invisibility has no
relationship to racism ("il ne s'agit pas ici d'une réaction
raciste"), being rather a manifestation of universal deper-
sonalization.   The reader picking his way between Messrs.
Sainville and Brodin/Dommergues, might justifiably wonder
whether they are talking about the same book.

The second survey book in the "Que Sais-Je?" series,
Jacques-Fernand Cahen's La littérature américaine, 5th updated version (1968), cannot even be accused of misrepresentation, for its only mention of Ellison occurs in a list
of writers emerging between 1945 and 1960.   Quite skimpy
in general, and even more so in its handling of black authors,
the book is apparently quite popular, judging from its several revisions and from the fact of its use in translation in
Germany as well.

In 1967, Pierre Dommergues published another book
entitled Les USA à la recherche de leur identité:  rencontres
avec 40 écrivains américains, which became an instant success.   Rather than a critical study, this is a series of col-
lages involving generous excerpts from the published writings
of each of the 40 authors included, and from interviews with
the compiler, followed by a brief section of comments on
each author by his contemporaries.   To the obvious difficulty posed by excerpts which are inevitably out of context,
is added the total lack of references, making it impossible
to track down any of the readings.   Dommergues' aim is to

allow his material total autonomy, but the fluidity of these "encounters" is undercut by his method of selection and organization, which often lock his subjects into rigid categories. This is especially true of the section devoted to black writers, where the three "rencontres" are arranged and captioned as follows: James Baldwin, "Libérer les blancs" ("Liberate whites"); LeRoi Jones, "Détruire l'Amérique" ("Destroy America"); Ralph Ellison, "L'intégration de l'esprit" ("The integration of the spirit"); clearly a thesis-oriented arrangement and one which reflects the priority of political over cultural considerations.

As he has stated elsewhere[9] Dommergues regards Ellison as representing on a cultural plane what he hopes will be the future in race relations--a subsuming of self-conscious negritude into a consciousness of one's total humanity. But this interpretation is not spelled out anywhere in Les USA .... And while the copious excerpts from S & A printed here would be informative to a thoughtful reader, they are equally subject to misinterpretation and oversimplification, as is the caption itself, from which one can easily extract the word "integration" as a convenient label. In any case, Dommergues' approach becomes a pace-setter: few scholars henceforth discuss Ellison without first going through the obligatory "confrontation" of him with LeRoi Jones. Les USA ... has undeniable merits in presenting the French reader with an updated and broad sample of Ellison's thinking; on the other hand it can easily be misconstrued, and the lack of scholarly apparatus (sketchy biography, no bibliography, erroneous listing of a purported 1967 French translation of I.M.) would make it difficult to pursue the subject further in serious study.

With Marc Saporta's 1970 Histoire du roman américain, one finds the beginning of the kind of closer study heretofore missing. Saporta, who in 1963 apparently did not consider black writers as participants in American literature (see note 4), comes late to Afro-American writers, and his chapter on them lacks the depth of the rest of his book; but he has at least done his homework--he provides information not available elsewhere (e.g., the role of The Crisis in developing black writers), he knows and cites the work of black scholars, and gives the reader a systematic perspective of major trends in Afro-American writing. Thoughtful though the treatment of Ellison is, it is somewhat marred by weaknesses such as dogmatism (he is pronounced "the greatest of living black writers"), the tendency

to compare black writers only to each other, and the ag-
grandizement of Ellison at the expense of Wright.  But at
least the focus is somewhat more literary than sociological,
and the ubiquitous integration-separation, Ellison-Jones
scenario is considerably muted.

A chronological table at the end of the book is useful in listing for the first time one of Ellison's short stories.
Following, as it does, H. I. 's 1969 appearance, Saporta's
book offers the reader valuable information and help toward
further study.  It thus represents a considerable advance over
the books that preceded it.


IV.  PRINCIPAL REVIEWS


The single review following I. M. 's 1954 French translation (Marcel Moussy, LetN, June, 1954), is remarkably
ahead of its time in lucidity and breadth:  Moussy places
Ellison within the broad context of a postwar anti-Hemingway
revolt, draws upon his prose essays, and pinpoints the
novel's moral preoccupation with racism and stereotyping.

In contrast to its 1954 predecessor, the 1969 translation received numerous reviews; reflecting the historical
circumstances which meanwhile forcefully moved the black
presence into European consciousness, these reviews now
stress the novel's documentary implications.  (The reader
looking for a primarily literary evaluation of H. I. should
consult the excellent essay by Marcel Lemaire in Le Soir
de Bruxelles, October 22, 1969).  Before even dealing with
the novel, most of the reviewers feel it mandatory to ad-
dress themselves first to the controversy surrounding Ellison's personal stand on black power ideology.  Having re-
discovered him from a vantage point which offers a seven-
teen-year flashback to 1952 (the novel's original date of
publication), they invariably choose to represent the magni-
tude of the intervening changes through the simplistic but
dramatically effective device of contrasting Ellison (integration) and LeRoi Jones (separation).  (In many cases, the
comparison is in Ellison's favor, leading one to wonder
why, if his quiet voice is ostensibly preferable to Jones's
supposed "savagery and screams of rage" ["sauvagerie" and
"hurlements"], the latter should be so much better known in
France. )

The cue, and much of the material for this "confrontation" are taken from Pierre Dommergues' previously discussed book, <u>Les USA à la recherche de leur identité</u> (1967).
Dommergues himself develops this approach again in his essay in <u>Le Monde,</u> June 14, 1969 ("rising to confront Ralph
Ellison there looms the figure of LeRoi Jones, historical
materialization of Ras the Destroyer"[10]).  To the credit of
most reviewers, the term "integration" with respect to Ellison is used with an awareness of its complexity; a noteworthy exception is Anne Thinesse's "portrait"-review in
<u>FL,</u> August 11-17, 1969, which translates, "Is Ralph Elli-
son anything but an Uncle Tom who has made it?"

In discussing <u>H. I.</u> itself, the reviewers look for its
possible contribution toward resolving the integration-separation deadlock already foreshadowed in it and now become a
reality.  The novel's commitment to intellectual lucidity as
a goal superseding ideologies impresses most reviewers
forcefully in this particular time of ideological conflicts.
Interestingly, the two dissenting voices from this view
argue from totally opposite standpoints:  Matthieu Galey,
<u>PP,</u> May 29, 1969, considers the book dated, and the time
for solitary underground mediation long superseded; Robert
Merle, in his translator's preface offers the original thesis
that far from aiming to transcend ideologies, Ellison is a
total participant in an ideological war; Merle reads <u>H. I.</u> as
a covert instrument of militancy and as a direct and ironic
contradiction of all Ellison's public "integrationist" statements.  The documentary stress of this essay, together
with its almost total omission of any literary considerations
(such as idiomatic problems encountered in the translation
process), is symptomatic of a prevailing imbalance in the
responses to black literary creativity.

It must be admitted, however, that the persistent
attention directed to the novel's concrete realities does give
the French reviewers a considerable edge over their American colleagues of 1952.  When <u>H. I.</u> is praised in terms almost echoing those of 1952--"a very great documentary"
(Annie Copperman, <u>Les Echos</u>), "a masterpiece" (Pierre
Kyria, <u>Combat</u>), "the greatest American Negro novel"
(Jacques Cabau, <u>L'Express</u>)--the similarity is only superficial, for much sharper thematic perceptions are now
brought into play; hindsight even allows a sense of compla-
cency in being able to point out, as Michèle Coté does, that
Americans missed the whole essence of the book, failing to
comprehend what it was they were so innocently acclaiming
in 1952.

H. I. 's trenchant analysis of racism is one major
dimension of which reviewers are strongly aware.  They
find the consequences of racism revealed even in matters of
form, as it modifies the novel's "Education Sentimentale"
mold, and causes the literary blueprint of the picaresque
success story to disintegrate upon contact with the protagonist's blackness.  The thematic manifestations of racism are
equally ubiquitous to these reviewers, and most ironically
so in what they recognize as the unwitting fratricide of the
final castration scene:

> In refusing to acknowledge the solidarity of Blacks
> and Whites, the executioners are condemning them-
> selves to disaster:  in castrating him, it is them-
> selves they are emasculating, and their denial of
> him is a rejection of themselves.  The book ends
> upon this positive note affirming a humanity ulti-
> mately discovered, but not yet universally acknowl-
> edged. [11]
> --Françoise Barrière, LetF, p. 4

As everyone knows, I. M., in addition to affirming
the principle of historical interdependence, is in its very
texture an exemplary demonstration of black and white
American cultural symbiosis, a fact which went largely unnoticed in America until the late 1960's.  Here again, the
French reviewers are able to offer insights conspicuously
absent from American reviews.  To the by now familiar
analysis of the book's American themes and techniques is
added a typically French twist, wherein the book's very defects are ascribed to nationality:  its many kinds of physical
and psychological violence are interpreted as manifestations
of that notorious "American style" which reflects America's
shortcomings; and if violence, rather than feeling serves as
a major rite of passage, the fault is in the culture rather
than in the author:

> Here, as often in the American novel, an op-
> erative cannibalism replaces the education of
> the feelings.  Violence substitutes itself for
> sexuality. [12]
> --Pierre Dommergues, Le Monde, p. IV

Another dividend of close reading is the exclusion of
hasty interpretations such as the popular "universalist" explication of the novel as a general protest against the metaphysical diminution of everyman's self.  Ellison's wide-

ranging Western erudition, as well as the French title of
I. M., pointing as it does to a question tentatively answered
in the book's final sentence ("Homme invisible, pour qui
chantes-tu?" ... "Qui sait si, dans des frequences trop
basses, je ne parle pas pour vous?"13) all seem to invite
precisely that kind of reading.   Perhaps Merle's brisk
quashing of this approach in his preface serves to warn
off subsequent readers:   citing William Goyen who sees the
invisible protagonist as a representative of contemporary
youth seeking its identity, Merle with deftly pointed logic
exposes the fallacy of this interpretation.

> William Goyen forgets--can this lapse be entirely
> involuntary?--that the protagonist is Black, and
> that consequently, his quest cannot be miraculously
> broadened to serve as an exemplary and typical
> model of the quest of all young boys and girls in
> the United States.   Skin pigmentation and resulting
> second class status in one's own country are
> things which can neither be glossed over nor trans-
> formed into a 'spiritual adventure.'14
> --"Preface," H. I., p. 10

One regrets that Merle's argument comes too late
to counter the very broad interpretations of I. M. offered
earlier by such authors of literary histories as Pierre
Brodin and Pierre Dommergues (see section III above).
Where reviewers do recognize the book's broader dimensions
(e. g., Jacques Cabau), the protagonist's blackness rather
than being fortuitous is recognized as a fact of central symbolic significance, an approach deriving perhaps from the
new tendency to see in the Negro the "black mask of humanity."

Just as the book's technique seems to be taken for
granted, matters such as style, internal coherence, vivid
characterization and incident, humor, and a memorable mixture of tones being noted more or less in passing, so one
finds relatively little serious criticism of it.   Michèle Coté
complains that the ending is contrived and pathetic, avoiding
the original problem raised in the book.   Other, and generally minor criticisms, deal with the Brotherhood (Pierre
Dommergues feels it was too facilely identified with the
Communist Party in America, while Françoise Barrière,
accepting the identification, feels Ellison treated the Party
too harshly), and with Ras, whom Pathé Diagne (PA, 1970)
sees as a simplistic caricature.

In sum, the French reader is offered in these reviews a perspective which, though inescapably marked by
the political conflicts of the moment, yet avoids most of
the mistakes and simplifications of early American responses,
confronts the book more directly, and suggests something
of the complex interweaving of its issues.


## V.  CRITICAL STUDIES


So far, very little has been done on Ellison in
French-language journals.   The earliest essay available
dates from 1961, nine years after I.M.'s original publication; all but two studies have reference only to American
editions of Ellison's work and the approach taken is uni-
formly sociological.   In spite of its limitations this material does offer honest and provocative insights, and is
especially interesting in its self-conscious feeling of superi-
ority over the sensibilities of most American critics.

Two essays by the American-born scholar Albert
Gérard, one in French, RGB (October, 1961), and one in
English, Diogenes (Spring, 1962), develop the thesis that
I.M. articulates the black man's postwar political dilemma
and foreshadows its resolution.   Further, Gerard sees this
novel as illustrating a predominant quality of black fiction:
while "putting white civilization on trial," this fiction also
"offers in action a series of values which the white world
has long yearned for, and which, in effect, constitute the
humanism of the future."   The values in question are "emotional personalism ... the natural integration of the personality, spontaneous spirituality."   Yet Gerard follows this
analysis of I.M.'s insights by nonetheless placing the novel
within the (for him) outworn protest tradition, expressing
the hope that Ellison will someday write about the new times
and abandon protest in favor of articulating the full range
of positive black values.

Pierre Dommergues, whose 1967 Les USA à la
recherche de leur identité is to become so influential,
analyzes America's racial problems in Le Monde, April 13,
1966.   On the cultural plane he sees Ellison, whom he
describes as practically unknown in France, representing
a stage of development that supersedes Jones's aggressive

declaration of negritude, by including black self-conscious-
ness into a broader consciousness of human identity.

   Robert Merle, the translator of I.M., offers in his
preface to H.I. yet another and strikingly original view of
Ellison which goes counter to appraisals of him as mired
in protest, or as a ripe humanist standing above the fray.
Merle, in fact, sees two Ellisons in action: one is the man
who appears in Dommergues' Les USA ... declaring that
"color is an accident," and, further (preposterously in
Merle's view), that blacks are in reality white--"en réalité,
nous sommes blancs comme les autres," i.e., the man who
is publicized for conciliatory and "integrationist" statements;
in total contrast to this public figure is the author of I.M.
whose novel adds up, as Merle sees it, to an indictment of
integration and to a realization of the impossibility of making
common cause or even conducting a dialog with white liberals
("le combat au côté des blancs, même libéraux, n'est pas
possible, le dialogue non plus"). Taken together, Ellison's
covert militancy, side by side with his overt integrationism,
constitute for Merle a spectacular display of subversion in
the spirit of the invisible protagonist's grandfather.

   Provocative as is Merle's thesis, it is disconcerting
to find that the novel's interest and value are for him linked
so exclusively to the extent of its demonstrable militancy.
The essay is, however, among the most thorough of all
French language studies, and deserves careful attention.

   Noteworthy for its outspoken honesty is an essay by
an American critic, John H. Randall, III in RLV (Brussels),
1965. The author insists on the specific relevance of I.M.
to the American scene, on the interrelatedness of black and
white as spelled out in the castration scene and in the
major metaphor of running, [15] and most of all on the ironic
paradox that these vital subjects went unrecognized in American literary circles when, in his view,

> If we ever do get around to having a twenty-first
> century, Ralph Ellison may be one of the men we
> can thank for having made us see ourselves as we
> really are, and thus for having helped us to sur-
> vive. (p. 44)

   The interdependence of black and white cultures is
argued also by Pierre-Yves Petillon, Critique (1968). His
thesis is that the current generation of black writers are the

unacknowledged true spiritual heirs of the great nineteenth
century writers like Hawthorne, Melville, Emerson and
Thoreau, and that the experiences they articulate are the
embodiment of American archetypal experience.[16] In I.M.,
for example, he finds basic American concerns:  the shat-
tering of an ossified universe to bring forth a world of new
possibilities, the impulse to preserve an open area for experience, to discover a radical "I," and to "tell it like it
is."  This being so, the exploration of black culture which
in fact is America's new frontier may lead to new dimensions of biracial self-discovery:  the black reader per-
ceiving his blackness within his American roots, the white
reader scrutinizing his country through black eyes and able
thus to trace the missing dimensions of his own features.
I.M. thus offers vital and as yet unrecognized possibilities
to its readers.

Guy Ducornet's 1969 lengthy discussion of I.M.
(LanM), is the only study available after the publication of
H.I.  This article is noteworthy for its scholarly approach
and skillful linking of I.M. with Ellison's prose essays from
1945 to 1961, thus conveying an all too rarely found sense
of the congruence and development of Ellison's major artistic concerns.  Close study of Ellison also enables Ducornet
to note some major shortcomings in the novel's American
reviews of 1952 and 1953:  among the major elements
missed were the fact that it was the quintessential American quest which I.M. was expressing through a black par-
ticularity, the complex and pervasive uses of humor, and
thus the whole presence of a black consciousness with ambivalent feelings about life in white America.  Ducornet
also argues against the conditioning which leads readers to
expect bitterness, brutality and revolt in black writing and
which might prevent them from justly appraising a book like
H.I.; in passing, he notes the current avalanche of black-
authored books whose quality is often disproportionate to
their quantity.

The French-language student of Ellison will find himself short on documentation, but in these studies he will at
least enjoy a thoughtful introduction to his author.

## Notes

1.   The Order was instituted by ministerial decree on May
     2, 1957, to reward those persons, French as well as

foreign, who "have distinguished themselves through
artistic and literary creativity, or through their contributions to the dissemination of arts and letters in
France and in the world." ("L'ordre des Arts et des
lettres est destiné à récompenser les personnes qui
se sont distinguées par leurs créations dans le do-
maine artistique ou littéraire ou par la contribution
qu'elles ont apportée au rayonnement des arts et des
lettres en France et dans le monde." Article 2,
decree 57-549, Journal Officiel, May 3, 1957, p.
4568.) It is administered by the Minister for Cultural Affairs, in 1968 the writer André Malraux,
whom Ellison has held in highest regard since the
1930's. By decree of October 21, 1968, Ellison was
named to the first of the order's three ranks (these
are, in ascending order, chevalier, officier, and
commandeur). The actual presentation was made at
the French Embassy in New York on February 25,
1969, but the information reached neither the New
York Times, nor Le Monde, appearing only in a few
lines in the France-Amérique.

2.  See Roger Asselineau, "Les américains sont-ils vrai-
ment américains?" Critique, 16, no. 157 (June, 1960),
483-495.

3.  The French taste apparently runs to the masochistic:
their pantheon of the "great" American writers consists of those who are said to strike the reader as
with "un coup de poing en pleine figure" ("a fist
smashed into one's face")--Caldwell, Steinbeck,
Dreiser, Hemingway and Faulkner, but not Melville,
Hawthorne, or James. The taste for this sort of
writing fluctuates considerably, having reached a peak
in the postwar years and a nadir in the fifties; and
while there are indications of an attack on the whole
myth of a simplistic, brutal America, its hold is yet
strong. The interested reader should consult some
of the following sources: Thelma M. Smith and
Ward L. Miner, Transatlantic Migration: the Contemporary American Novel in France, Durham, N.C.:
Duke University Press, 1955; Claude Edmonde Magny,
L'age du roman américain, Paris: Editions du Seuil,
1948; "Traduit de l'américain," La Parisienne, no.
43 (April, 1957), 468-472; Pierre Brodin, Présences
contemporaines: écrivains américains d'aujourd'hui
des années 50, Paris, Nouvelles Editions Demeresse,

1964; Marcel Brion, "Un panorama de la littérature
américaine," La Revue, 15 (March, 1955), 351; G.
Remords, "Les lettres américaines et la critique
universitaire française," BFLS, 35, no. 3 (December, 1956), 160-177 and Michel Mohrt, Le nouveau
roman américain, Paris: Gallimard, 1955.

4.   See Europe, 37, nos. 358-359 (February-March, 1959);
     in this special issue devoted to American literature,
     the chronological table of major political and literary
     events lists James Michener (1947) and Herman Wouk
     (1950), but not Ralph Ellison or James Baldwin.   Cf.
     also Marc Saporta, "Autoportrait de la littérature
     américaine," I&D, no. 187 (15 September-1 October,
     1963); not a single black writer is included in this
     strangely one-dimensional "autoportrait." This same
     journal waited until 1968 to inform its readers that
     Ellison was an American author worth serious con-
     sideration.   The Grand Larousse (1961) devotes one
     single sentence to Afro-American literature within its
     discussion of the American novel, and Wright's is the
     only name mentioned.   Ironically, Roger Asselineau
     (see n. 2), who doubts the existence of a distinct
     American culture, considers only its Negro component
     to be original, but he specifically excludes belles-
     lettres from this judgment, which relates to "folk"
     creativity only.

5.   Formerly a USIA publication, now issued by Services
     américains d'information et de relations culturelles
     in Paris.

6.   "Is Ralph Ellison anything but an Uncle Tom who has
     made it?"

7.   As late as 1969, Raymond Las Vergnas, also a well-
     known critic, uses a very similar approach; on the
     basis of Richard Wright's and James Baldwin's novels
     (Ellison is not mentioned), he draws the general con-
     clusion that Afro-American writing now transcends
     the "simple" conflict between blacks and whites, in
     favor of metaphysical meditation in situations where
     "human beings are alike in relation to infinity" ("les
     êtres humains sont semblables au regard de l'infini").
     "Images du roman américain d'aujourd'hui," Les
     Annales, 79 (June, 1969), 16.

8. "Homme Invisible est un livre très fort, qui laisse au
   lecteur l'impression d'avoir été soulevé par un bulldozer" (p. 57).

9. Pierre Dommergues, Le Monde, April 13, 1966. Reprinted as "Le problème noir aux Etats-Unis," LanM,
   60, no. 3 (May-June, 1966), 326-330.

10. "en face de Ralph Ellison se dresse la silhouette de
    LeRoi Jones, matérialisation historique de Ras,
    l'Exhorteur."

11. En refusant de reconnaître que Noirs et Blancs sont
    solidaires, les bourreaux se condamnent à la catas-
    trophe: en le castrant, ils se castrent eux-mêmes,
    en le niant, c'est eux-mêmes qu'ils nient. Le livre
    s'achève sur cette affirmation d'une humanité enfin
    trouvée mais non reconnue encore.

12. Ici, comme souvent dans le roman américain, un canni-
    balisme efficace remplace l'éducation sentimentale.
    La violence se substitue à la sexualité.

13. "Who knows, but that, on the lower frequencies, I speak
    for you?"

14. "William Goyen oublie (mais l'oubli est-il tout à fait
    involontaire?) qu'il s'agit d'un Noir et que sa quête
    ne saurait donc être, par miracle, étendue--exem-
    plaire et typique--à 'tous les jeunes, garçons et
    filles,' des Etats-Unis. S'il y a quelque chose qui
    ne se laisse pas gommer, ni transformer en 'aven-
    ture spirituelle,' c'est la pigmentation de la peau et
    le statut de citoyen de seconde zone dans son propre
    pays." Goyen's remarks appeared in Dommergues,
    Les USA ..., pp. 423-424, as part of a projected
    study on Ellison which is still unpublished.

15. "All through the book it seems to be the Negro who is
    running, but by the time you finish you discover that
    the white people are doing much more running and
    are hurting themselves much more by doing so.
    They are running because they are using violence
    against others in order not to face the anguish and
    travail of the birth of self-knowledge." (p. 44)

16. "... la génération noire actuelle est en train de refaire,

cent ans plus tard, l'expérience exemplaire de la
grande génération anglo-saxonne de 1840.   C'est elle
qui recuille le vrai héritage américain de Hawthorne,
Melville, Emerson et Thoreau et non pas les Anglo-
Saxons, aujourd'hui enkystés dans leurs banlieues
après avoir oublié, laissé pourrir ce qui faisait
l'originalité de l'Amérique. "

("The current black generation is reliving,
one hundred years later, the exemplary experience
of the great Anglo-Saxon generation of 1840.   It is
this generation which has appropriated the true American heritage of Hawthorne, Melville, Emerson and
Thoreau, not today's Anglo-Saxons, cocooned as they
are in their suburbs, after having forgotten, having
allowed to rot, that which constituted the originality
of America. ") (p. 860)

GERMANY - ESSAYS

# INTRODUCTION

Of the three European countries surveyed, Germany is the most hospitable to Ellison, and strangely enough, more so in the early 1950's than in the late 1960's.

S. Fischer Verlag first published the German translation of I. M. (entitled Unsichtbar) in 1954, then reissued it in 1969. Upon its first appearance, the book seems to have created a mild sensation: it attracted reviews in fifty publications, a record number which in fact surpasses even the notice given I. M. on its home grounds in 1952--and this in a country whose population at the time was roughly one-third that of the U. S. To this should be added reviews in Austrian and German-Swiss papers, and at least three German radio broadcasts, one of them an adaptation of the novel, to get an idea of the wide exposure enjoyed by the book. Even the reissue of 1969 attracted quite a respectable number of reviews, and an additional radio discussion. It goes without saying that the majority of reviewers seem remarkably well-informed and that they assume an equal degree of sophistication in their readership.

In the fall of 1954, perhaps partly in the wake of the encouraging response to Unsichtbar, S. Fischer arranged a joint tour of major German cities (Ulm, Frankfurt, Köln, among others) for Ellison and the young German author, Paul Schallück. Of this combination, critic Wolfgang Ebert wrote approvingly: "Whatever else may separate them-- they have in common the search for a way out of the wretchedness and despair which have hitherto characterized new writing."[1] The partnership seems in any case to have been a congenial one, for Schallück (whose new book coincidentally bore the title The Invisible Gate) displayed great energy in publicizing his American colleague, reviewing Unsichtbar at great length, adapting it for broadcast, and speaking to German audiences about it.

It is thus fair to say that Ellison's introduction to
the German public was a most auspicious one.  This degree
of consideration is the more remarkable, as it seems to go
counter to a longstanding disparaging German attitude toward America and its culture.  At its crassest, the popular
notion sees the U. S. as a world "of fantastic success
stories ... gangsterism, and somewhere on the periphery
despair, misery, utter loneliness; and next to it, immatur-
ity, naiveté, lack of culture."[2]  This myth with its under-
tones of envy results from a reading of America's "hardboiled" writers, who until the early 1950's, and in spite of
the German "discovery" and admiration for Faulkner, Wilder,
O'Neill and Wolfe, were still regarded as offering typical
representations of their country.  At one point, many young
writers even considered this style and approach as eminently
worthy of emulation.  But perhaps Ellison proves so fas-
cinating precisely because he so manifestly explodes these
myths in his work as well as in his person, thus answering
the needs of those who had been working in increasing numbers since 1945 to reappraise America realistically.[3]  Whatever the circumstances, it seems evident that by 1954 many
German literati are ready to welcome a new kind of American literature, one whose truth resides not in materialism,
brutality and despair, but rather in those human qualities
extolled by Faulkner in his oft-quoted Nobel prize speech
of 1950 as the proper province of the arts.

> I decline to accept the end of man.... I believe
> that man will not merely endure:  he will prevail.
> He is immortal, not because he alone among
> creatures has an inexhaustible voice, but because
> he has a soul, a spirit capable of compassion and
> sacrifice and endurance.  The poet's, the writer's,
> duty is to write about these things.  It is his
> privilege to help man endure by lifting his heart,
> by reminding him of the courage and honor and
> hope and pride and compassion and pity and sacri-
> fice which have been the glory of his past.  The
> poet's voice need not merely be a record of man,
> it can be one of the props, the pillars to help
> him endure and prevail.[4]

Unsichtbar seems to echo perfectly this spirit of
universality, optimism, energy, positive thinking, and
metaphysical self-assertion which is the new desideratum.
Indeed, in Ellison's own acceptance speech at the National
Book Award presentation ceremony, the German reviewers

find a formulation of aims to which they can only give their
warmest assent.   There is thus considerable predisposition
to praise Unsichtbar on conceptual grounds, let alone for
its execution.   And in justice to the reviewers, they work
hard to meet the book upon its own terms, a process which
renders superficiality almost impossible.   Patronizing of
Ellison as a black man is almost in total abeyance (with
some marked exceptions).

While Ellison unquestionably struck a responsive
chord immediately upon his appearance, the aftermath of
his German career seems disappointingly meager:   none of
the excitement generated in the early reviewers is reflected
in the Ellison entries in reference works; hardly any of his
other writings have been translated into German, and even
the number of critical studies is small (with a large proportion of Marxist-oriented work).   Undeserved dust is
thus--temporarily one hopes--gathering around his pedestal.


## I.  BIOGRAPHICAL INFORMATION

While the brief entries on Ellison in major reference
works contribute some errors--such as the description of
S & A as a novel and of I. M. as semi-autobiographical--they
provide hardly any factual information beyond dates of birth
and of I. M. 's publication.   A good but ephemeral source
is the "portrait" which appeared in Zeit during Ellison's
lecture tour in September of 1954.

To date the most informative German source on
Ellison's life remains a fifteen-year-old essay by Heinz
Rogge (NS, 15, 1958) where ample biographical detail is
interwoven into the literary discussion.


## II.  BIBLIOGRAPHIES

No primary bibliography is available to the German
student.

88 The Blinking Eye

Two sources list secondary material: <u>Kindlers Lit-</u>
<u>eratur Lexikon</u> (Zürich, 1964) confines its list to eight
American essays, all authored by white scholars.   The second source, Gerhard H. W. Zuther's <u>Bibliographie</u> ..., a
compilation of materials documenting the postwar German
reaction to American literature (1965), offers a unique bibliography of German sources, including author bibliographies.
His only limitations with respect to Ellison are his relatively
early cutoff date of 1960, and his exclusion of daily and
weekly newspapers.

After 1960, the reader finds no organized tools to
help in compiling a bibliography.


III.   REFERENCE WORKS AND LITERARY HISTORIES


The Ellison entries in German reference works deal
only with <u>I. M.</u> and range from brief summaries such as
provided in Johannes Beer's <u>Romanführer</u> (1969), to the
broad and penetrating analysis found in <u>Kindlers Literatur</u>
<u>Lexikon</u> as early as 1964.   Somewhere in between are the
several entries in <u>Lexikon der Weltliteratur im 20. Jahr-</u>
<u>hundert</u> (1959/1961).   Here, both the individual Ellison entry
and the discussion of Ellison in the essay on American literature (written by Britisher Geoffrey Moore) have a slightly patronizing flavor, interspersing praise of Ellison with qualifications about his subjectivity (the novel is described as the fruit
of excessive and aggressive sensitivity) and on the low level of
achievement in the black novel in general (on the whole, Moore
says, black writers, regrettably, still produce stereotyped
characters and propaganda).

Few of the literary histories examined do more than
simply refer to Ellison as a writer of international repute.
He is omitted entirely from <u>American Civilization,</u> an inter-
nationally edited handbook for American studies published in
London in 1968.   Here the chapter on American literature
was provided by Heinrich Straumann, Swiss scholar and
author of <u>American Literature in the Twentieth Century</u>
(1951), a popular book judging by its several reissues in
1962 and 1965, wherein short shrift is given to black
authors.   Other noteworthy examples of omission include
John V. Hagopian and M. Dolch, eds., <u>Insight I:   Analyses</u>

of American Literature (1962), a textbook for use in German
schools, and Elizabeth Schnack's anthology, Amerikanische
Erzähler (1957), the latter claiming to offer the reader an
image of America and its people while neglecting to include
even a single black writer.

   Those literary histories which do recognize and discuss Ellison applaud him primarily for transcending the protest tradition.  See notably Martin Schulze, Wege der amerikanischen Literatur (1968), and John Brown's Panorama der
modernen Literatur U. S. A. (1964), a translation of the
American author's original French book.  A Marxist perspective is expressed in Karl Heinz Schönfelder's and Karl
Heinz Wirzberger's Amerikanische Literatur im Uberblick
(Leipzig, 1968), one of the few books offering the reader a
bibliography of materials for the study of Afro-American literature.  While Unsichtbar is praised on a formal level, it
is, predictably, considered a failure, inasmuch as it leaves
no room for constructive action.  Moreover, Ellison's and
Baldwin's alleged "pessimism" and uncertainty about the future are attributed to their middle-class perspective and to
their lack of interest in the black masses.


## IV.  PRINCIPAL REVIEWS


### 1954

   Unsichtbar, Georg Goyert's translation of I. M. , published by S. Fischer in 1954, was greeted with some excitement in the German press, garnering an impressive
fifty reviews, many of them in the leading papers such as
Die Welt, Die Zeit, Frankfurter Allgemeine Zeitung, and
Süddeutsche Zeitung.  (Additional reviews appear in the
Austrian and German-Swiss press and will be briefly discussed at the end of the present section. )  Aware of the
book's success in America, yet judging it independently
from their own point of view, the majority of reviewers
unhesitatingly endorse Unsichtbar as an impressive first
novel.  This judgment is not rendered uncritically:  comments such as "extraordinary, " "splendid, " "an almost
frighteningly good piece of literature, " "a miraculous blend
of form and theme, " "an achievement upon the pinnacle of
American narrative art, "[5] notwithstanding, the reader is
regularly and explicitly alerted to the novel's weaknesses.

Ellison was correct in his judgment that "the Germans, having no special caste assumptions concerning American Negroes, dealt with my work simply as a novel,"[6] for most of the German criticism (and its Swiss and Austrian counterparts) may be described as open, fair-minded, and alert to the dangers of its own ignorance.    There are, however, some exceptions, and these are of such an unpleasant nature that their impact is out of all proportion to their numbers, almost sufficient to mar the favorable impression of the whole.

German receptivity to Unsichtbar seems to rest quite as much upon what the novel is not, as upon what it is. Sighs of relief are almost audible as the reviewers discover the book's calculated abandon of the customary pattern of its twin sources--the recent American novel, and the "Negro" novel.  Rephrased in positive terms, the critics hail in Unsichtbar a new trinity of approaches which, though overlapping, may be identified as the blending of realism and mythic imagination in form and technique, the modulation from the specific to the universal in thrust, and the execution of these by means of a rich, highly original compound of styles.    Though the performance may occasionally fall short of the intent, the intent itself deserves major credit in the reviewers' opinion, for rerouting narrative art into a fertile and long overdue new direction.

It is with Ellison's own words that the reviewers begin their interpretive journey through Unsichtbar.  Given generous citations from Ellison's acceptance speech at the National Book Award presentation ceremony, the reader thus has the artist's, rather than the critic's perspective before him at the very outset.    Laudable as this approach is, its ubiquitousness does produce excessive uniformity. In spite of the seeming disparities implied by such titles as "A Black Everyman," "A Novel of Utmost Resignation," "Damned to Perpetual Optimism,"[7] the reviews as a whole are disconcertingly homogeneous, agreeing on most major points and differing only in degree of intensity and in writing skill.

Key passages from Ellison's speech follow:

> ... if I were asked in all seriousness just what
> I considered to be the chief significance of In-
> visible Man as a fiction, I would reply:  Its ex-
> perimental attitude, and its attempt to return to

the mood of personal moral responsibility for
democracy which typified the best of our nineteenth-century fiction ... to see America with an
awareness of its rich diversity and its almost
magical fluidity and freedom, I was forced to con-
ceive of a novel unburdened by the narrow naturalism which has led, after so many triumphs, to the
final and unrelieved despair which marks so much
of our current fiction.   I was to dream of a prose
which was flexible, and swift as American change
is swift, confronting the inequalities and brutal-
ities of our society forthrightly, but yet thrusting
forth its images of hope, human fraternity and individual self-realization.   It would use the richness
of our speech, the idiomatic expression and the
rhetorical flourishes from past periods which are
still alive among us.   And despite my personal
failures, there must be possible a fiction which,
leaving sociology to the scientists, can arrive at
the truth about the human condition, here and now,
with all the bright magic of a fairy tale.

> --"Brave Words for a Startling
> Occasion," in S & A, pp.
> 111, 113.

As will be noted, this passage expresses all three of the
new approaches which the German critics find so congenial.
First and foremost is the aim to arrive at truth "with all
the bright magic of a fairy tale," apparently a welcome departure to those tired of "hardboiled," "realistic" American
writing with its fatal attraction to young German authors.
"How fortunate would it be for German literature," says the
reviewer for the FV, "if one could find a book written within the last few years even remotely capable of blending so
much imagination with such rational thinking."[8]  Realism
such as Ellison's, which presents itself decently draped
in soul, allows the reader to feel "uplifted," without the
sense of having been cheated of the "truth."   Paul Schallück,
himself a novelist, eloquently sums up what he and his colleagues relish in Unsichtbar's approach to the world.

> Over the whole novel there hovers the breath of a
> fairy tale, in spite of the harshest realism;
> through it there sounds the echo of an ancient song,
> which is ours, yet unknown to us and therefore
> inexpressible.   In critical jargon one would say:
> this novel is a work of poetry.[9]

Unsichtbar's sense of humor, largely unnoticed by
early American reviewers and here described as "gütiger
Humor,"--"genial" or "kindly" humor--is often pointed out
as effective in maintaining the book's balance of contraries
and in finally allowing the kind of ultimate faith in man
which the Germans admired so highly in Faulkner.  "In
spite of its harshness, the awful, cruel reality is not devoid
of the kindliness of humor and the warmth of humanity,"[10]
writes the reviewer for HP.  Closer to hand, Ellison's
novel approach also enlightens by its unique image of American reality:

> America has been lauded to the skies and it has
> been mercilessly denounced.  But never yet have
> we heard a voice such as Ellison's.  His image of
> America is wrested piece by piece from the most
> bitter experiences, yet filled out nonetheless with
> light and shadow.  Literarily, humanly and po-
> litically, a first rate book.[11]

The second area of critical appreciation--the organic
growth of the general out of the specific--is the corollary
of Ellison's concern to balance the "real" and the "imaginary."
Repeatedly, Ellison is praised for not getting "bogged down"
in racial protest, and for moving beyond race into the realm
of the "allgemein menschliches" (the "universally human").
This response is familiar from American reviews, yet with
a difference:  in Germany, the book's racial component is
neither obliterated nor diffused into vague generalizations;
indeed, for most reviewers, the book's "blackness" constitutes its vital core.  This is shown variously:  in Spiegel's
suggestion that a Negro's vision for racial and human problems is sharper than that of most whites who can still af-
ford their illusions; in Max Ruland's contention (MM) that
the book arrives at universal truths precisely by being so
thoroughly immersed in its own subjective reality of race
prejudice; or in the admiration with which several writers
view America's "enlightenment" in bestowing the distinction
of the National Book Award upon an author who so com-
pellingly brings to light the shortcomings of white society.
(Here one may argue that the German critics overestimate
American comprehension of the book.  The French reviewers of 1969 are closer to the mark when they sense an
irony in the Award--America, they feel, knew not what it
was so innocently acclaiming.  An Austrian reviewer's
more cynical interpretation of the Award may be equally to
the point, but it is a minority of one amidst the general

optimism: "It remains to be seen, " speculates Helene
Ehmann (WZ), "whether the Award is an answer signifying
a readiness for the novel's question, or whether it is only
an ostentatious gesture in the service of newly arisen political necessities. "[12]

     Further evidence that blackness is confronted before
being embraced as part of universal humanity, is the occa-
sional confessed ignorance of the white critics, and their
hesitancy in appraising a book which in spite of the universality of art does spring out of so much experience alien
to them.  How honest such a self-appraisal can be is demonstrated in a penetrating essay by Monika von Zitzewitz in
Zeit.  In reviewing the European (and, for that matter,
American) image of the Negro, she realizes that in spite
of his many guises (athlete, musician, soldier), he has
never yet succeeded in penetrating the white consciousness
as other than the Noble Savage, that is to say, a figure
eliciting sentimentality but no authentic human response.
Unsichtbar, she feels, effectively demolishes these white
defenses, forcing its readers to confront the Negro as a
live human being, and to readjust their responses accord-
ingly.  Given the possibility of such an opening of white
minds, K. L. Tank reflects on the overlooked contributions
which black people can make to our understanding of them,
of America, and of humanity at large:

> For the first time, the Negro's revolutionary
> spiritual claims are here represented with such
> clarity, vigor and depth ... one may see from
> Ellison's book how much the Negro race has to
> offer us in terms of energy, spirituality, and a
> sharpening of conscience.  In this non-material
> sense, America once more becomes a continent
> of unbounded possibility. [13]

    Clearly these statements do not spring from minds
seeking to evade the mystery, power, and human ramifica-
tion of the black experience.  If they nonetheless look beyond it, they are responding to what they take to be Ellison's own ultimate quest for "the truth about the [total]
human condition. "

> ... dispassionately, he orders one image next
> to the other, draws realistically in ripe colors,
> avoids cheap sensationalism, is himself with
> every utterance, and depicts with unbroken vigor

situations which in their uniqueness of matter and
form take away the reader's breath.  And constantly he gropes his way nearer to the secret
which is man, seizes the elusive one repeatedly
and finally grasps him as the opposite of a god,
of a hero, a being at once good and evil, strong
and weak, black and white. 14

The third area, that of Unsichtbar's diction, flowing
as it does from the effort to show American "diversity and
swiftness of change, " receives almost uniform commendation.
Helmut Braem's assessment (StZ) may serve as a representative sample.

Ralph Ellison has herein chosen a path attempted
by Walt Whitman and later by Thomas Wolfe.  Yet
it is a new path, since it is always measured
anew by its own time.  This is the poetic endeavor
to allow one's own country to become incarnate in
language.  The success is as yet small, but already manifest.... And herewith Ralph Ellison
may lay claim to having set a milestone in American literary history. 15

These remarks highlight the German critics' sharp
eye for weaknesses as well as their appreciation for bold
innovative directions.  In spite of the fascination with Ellison's stylistic boldness, complaints about excessive wordiness and occasionally uncontrolled rhetoric are common.
Indeed, Thilo Koch suggested over Free Berlin radio that
Ellison would have done well to imitate Hemingway's rejected style and condense his work to its essentials.  Jürgen Eyssen (BB) notes in addition a tendency toward uniformity of tone, with a consequent weakening of the possibility for exploiting subtle contrasts.  On the other hand,
R. Krämer-Badoni (DZ) complains of excessive senational-
ism included for the sake of bestsellerdom.

Given the ambitiousness of the stylistic undertaking,
the quality of the translation becomes all-important, but
those critics who do mention it seem divided in their opinions, some feeling that Goyert was precise as well as subtle,
others on the contrary finding his prose stilted and inadequate to its task.  Unfortunately, the book was not available for perusal.

The ending, and thus the general interpretation of the

novel's sense, is another area of mild reviewer disagreement and criticism.   There is some feeling that the novel
ends in resignation, in a dead end, or at the very least in
uncertainty, but those readers are in a minority.   So is
the critique by the writer in FV that the ending is escapist
and lacks practicality, but this approach becomes much
more frequent in reviews of the late 1960's.

The perceptive openmindedness of most of the foregoing leaves one unprepared for some very curious regres-
sions to racism, by way of criticism of weaknesses which
are identified as racial rather than formal.   In terms of
numbers these instances are negligible, but in terms of
influence, appearing as they do in some of the leading newspapers and journals, they cannot be so easily dismissed.

The reviewer of WB, for example, feels that in
addition to its thin, unoriginal plot, the novel suffers from
excessively programmatic cerebration.   Had he read Paul
Schallück's enthusiastic involvement in Unsichtbar's implica-
tions--"we are the invisible ones ... we knew it but could
not pinpoint it ... a black man came and gave us our name.
We must thank him"[16]--it would seem totally alien to him;
for his part, he cannot bring himself to accept the metaphoric transformation of the "wretched Harlem reality" into
a truth valid for the white world: at most it is, he says, a
half-truth, lacking in illumination.   Race thus mars the
book's performance and limits its impact.   In addition, this
reviewer quotes at length and with apparent agreement from
a curious essay by Werner Helwig, of whom more presently.
Two other reviewers, K. H. Kramberg (SdZ) and Friedrich
Neuschaefer (TS), turn diagnosticians, alerting the reader
to the fact that Ellison's sensibilities are torn because of
racial resentments of which he may not even be consciously
aware, but which are clearly manifested in Unsichtbar, to
its detriment.   The unresolved conflict between racial
grudges and the desire to intellectualize about democratic
ideals, in Kramberg's view, keeps the work far short of
universality (while, on the other hand allowing stylistic innovations which flow from the exploitation of contradiction
and conflict).   Neuschaefer extends this argument even
further in companion reviews of Unsichtbar and Alan Paton's
Too Late the Phalarope.   Paton is described as "quite
simply great," whereas Ellison, being black, is crippled
by ambivalence:

In its ultimate spiritual core the book is a

> document of deep melancholy, not to say of art
> laced with despair and of resentment stylized as
> literature.   This perhaps only half-acknowledged
> and thus even more ambivalent posture may be the
> source of the book's spiritual and formal dichoto-
> my ... [17]

Dichotomy, because Neuschaefer feels the book misses its
mark; what should logically have been a relentless documentary is dissipated into labored, fuzzy allegory, so that
in spite of single brilliant poetic devices, the whole remains seriously flawed and incomplete.

        Most extreme is the preposterous essay by Werner
Helwig, appearing in what is perhaps the most prestigious
of all German papers, the FAZ.   Calling Unsichtbar "one
of the highest achievements of American narrative art, "
Helwig then proceeds to adjudge it a bastard, "a plant with
white blossoms and black roots, " and to pity its author as
"a staggering example of intellectual pauperization. "[18]
Here, Helwig reasons, is a writer who, without imitating,
has succeeded magnificently in portraying black experience
by means of the highest tools of white artistic expression.
Yet this brilliant adaptation of white devices underscores
all the more pathetically an irremediable deficiency of the
"Negro mind":

> The book seems to confirm ... that the Negro
> can put on our language and cultural dress, can
> even come to consider them as his own spiritual
> skin, but ... he will still lack our capacity to
> verbalize tensions.   This capacity cannot be
> learned. [19]

Lack of these "antibodies to chimeras" as Helwig elsewhere
calls them, leads Ellison as a black man into a despair
which is totally foreign to the white world; whites, he says,
have an inner sense of stability which regulates their relationships to each other and to the world, and which infuses
their art with emotional balance, as even the most somber
pages of a Faulkner or a Wolfe will attest.   (Miraculously,
the myth of American optimism is here stretched into a
universal "white" truth. )   The argument is clinched by evidence of a white man's brilliant success in the area of the
black man's failure:   South African writer Peter Lanham's
Blanket Boy's Moon is said to be a superb example of the
attempt "to describe black experience with the narrative

means of blacks. " Helwig's concluding judgment is that
Lanham offers the reader an artistic as well as practically
useful articulation of black African experience, while Ellison's work remains in the realm of limited literary significance.

We meet Mr. Helwig once again in the leading Swiss
paper, St. Galler Tagblatt, with his theories of white su-
periority intact, though rephrased. Here he benevolently
describes the Negro race sprinting to catch up in a few
decades to the things "we" took centuries to develop--civi-
lization, individualism, and the nihilism resulting there-
from. Ellison's book (which he judges to be autobiographical) dramatizes this marathon and its difficulties: the
protagonist is handicapped in equal measure by his problems
and by his racial inability to set up inner defenses against
them, as a white person would have done. Ellison's greatest achievement then, is the dramatization of this historic
process (which leads to a species of "black nihilism") in
the highest terms of white art. The review, ending with a
reference to Ellison as "this great poet of the contemporary
black experience, "[20] is again clearly intended to be com-
plimentary. But as the old saying goes, "with such friends,
who needs enemies?" That such explicitly racist assumptions can be offered and accepted as serious literary criticism gives one food for uncomfortable thought.

There remain for brief consideration the other Ger-
man-language reviews from Switzerland and Austria. They
are less numerous than their German counterparts, but once
again, the leading papers are well represented, for example
the Neue Zürcher Zeitung in Switzerland and the Salzburger
Nachrichten in Austria. On the whole, the reviewers are
sympathetic, and do not depart markedly from the main
lines of the German assessment. One exception is the
anonymous review in NZZ which is a strange mixture of
hostility, appreciation, and fantasy. The writer begins by
interpreting the National Book Award as evidence that
America in its zeal for honest self-appraisal particularly
values "rebellious blacks" such as Ellison. Next, he berates Ellison for his "presumptuous" rejection of Hemingway
which smacks of over-sensitivity and overcompensation.
Proceeding to the interpretation of Unsichtbar, he then
leaps feet first into the "biographical fallacy," expunging
the boundaries between Ellison and his protagonist, to blend
them into a freak "portrait" of today's black man.

> The now forty-year-old author was educated in a
> Negro college.  For the African that he had re-
> mained within, the learning of European-American
> wisdom did not last long....  From this point be-
> gins his flight--from Europe, from the whites,
> from himself--into the existence of an 'invisible
> man' and into the rejection of the whole world
> surrounding him....  The most treacherous disil-
> lusion is the one he experiences from ... the
> Brotherhood ... which he joins but which cannot at
> length tolerate him, just as he cannot tolerate it,
> he, the honest one acting primarily through enthu-
> siastic impulse, the forthright one, who in an im-
> portant sense is a primitive and an innocent. [21]

The review ends with an appreciation of Ellison's radical
search for human truth, which comes almost as a surprise
after the development of the rest of the essay.

As for the Austrian reviews, they incline in general
toward a direct reading of Unsichtbar as the expression of
racial problems.  The reviewers are impressed with the
difficulties depicted in the novel, and sensitive to its ironies.
In view of its maturity, the consensus is that for Europeans
this is a work valuable artistically as well as for its political information.

In sum, the reaction of the majority of German-
language reviewers may be described as a serious attempt
to confront Unsichtbar on its own terms, particularly as
these terms define such a welcome promise of narrative
regeneration.  As Axel Kaun (BK) writes,

> at a time when so many novels are superficial,
> glossy, vacuously affirmative or artificial, or
> form-and directionless, Unsichtbar deals with hu-
> man problems scarcely perceived by any other
> author; and this in a form and scope of extra-
> ordinary thoughtfulness which sets a new milestone
> in the development of literary art. [22]

### 1969-1970

Taking advantage of increased reader interest in Afro-
Americana, Fischer Verlag in the fall of 1969 reissued
Unsichtbar, adding the mod touch by depiction of a Black

Power fist on the cover. This second edition proved fairly
successful, with 900 copies sold in the next year and a
half.[23] Once again, the novel attracted a respectable number of reviews, including several from Austria and Switzerland; it was also the subject of a radio broadcast in Stutt-
gart on January 29, 1970.

On the whole, the responses are more cursory than
those of 1954, the book having by this time achieved undis-
puted status as an American classic. Its universality is
still deeply appreciated (for a particularly thoughtful discussion see Monika Blöcker's essay in the Swiss Profil), but
the nature of the times has brought about a major shift of
German critical perspective toward a reassessment of the
novel as a documentary. In a radical turnabout, "realism,"
the stone despised fifteen years earlier, is now the corner-
stone, with "imagination" become excess baggage. As one
might expect, the novel fares less well when measured by
a yardstick foreign to it, and the level of the discourse is,
in many cases, equally diminished.

Those reviewers who find documentary reality in
Unsichtbar are impressed by the book's lucidity (things have
not changed since 1952--IKZ), or shocked by its supposed
findings (according to Fritz Pilwachs, NV, the novel shows
black people still unsure of their aims and locked in a
vicious cycle of violence). Seen in retrospect, the novel's
expressed hope of racial reconciliation fixes for us the dimensions of a chance irretrievably lost (Anneliese Dempf,
Die Furche, Vienna, August 8, 1970). On a more symbolic level, the writer who notes that Ellison's theme of
invisibility is a traditional Afro-American concept which
only seemed original by reason of white ignorance, is also
implicitly arguing for the reality of Ellison's vision (Hansjürgen Rosenbauer, FR, January 17, 1970).

In sharp contrast with the foregoing we find arguments denying the novel's importance on the grounds that
it lacks contact with reality: taxed with subjectivity, irrationality, rhetorical distortion and lack of economy, it is,
incredibly, criticized for failing to arouse indignation along
the lines of Uncle Tom's Cabin and for rising into myth to
avoid the necessity of proposing concrete solutions (Gertrud
Huber, BZ). Another writer judges the book deficient by
virtue of historical untruth, sociological irrelevance, outdated stress on literary sublimation, and "white" thinking:
the book is not only imbued with American traditions, but

is also "from the first page to the last, a paraphrase of
Emerson's famous dictum about the 'general education of
the eye' "[24] (Jürgen Manthey, SdZ, November 29, 1969).
According to Manthey, radical blacks did not even bother
attacking the book, a sure sign of its irrelevance (ironically,
an even surer sign of the reviewer's ignorance writ large).

One element totally lacking from the German-lan-
guage reactions is the minute personal scrutiny of Ellison's
stand on the integration-separation issue which so exercised
the French critics.  But, by and large, the perspective of
the late 1960's seems to have provided new overlays of
rhetoric and political myth rather than additional knowledge
and more mature judgment.


## V.  CRITICAL STUDIES


The large majority of the essays in which Ellison is
discussed are devoted to the examination of broader topics,
such as contemporary Afro-American literature, the image of
the Negro, of society, or of urban civilization.  Inasmuch as
some of these essays appear to be American-authored
(though accurate identification is not always possible), cau-
tion is indicated in any generalization about "German"
scholarship.  On the other hand, the material again reveals
a broad homogeneity of basic assumptions, which can only
be explained by assuming fundamental agreement between
German and American critics, or else conscious sensitivity
by the latter toward the attitudes of the former.  A further
distinctive feature of these studies is the fact that a good
many of them are Marxist oriented.

The delineation of Negro characters in American fiction is the subject of several partly Marxist essays--see
Edward Clark, JAS, 1960, and Charles H. Nichols, SBV,
1960; JAS, 1961; NSM, 1965.  Ellison is here considered
by have pioneered in the creation of complex as well as
convincing Negro characters, a feat representing much more
than a welcome augury of racial progress; for in exploring
and rendering visible the Negro's humanity, Ellison has
made it paradigmatic, thus helping us rediscover our own.
The reader will be familiar with this variant of the "black
mask of humanity" theory.  What does take one by surprise,

in light of these assertions, is these and other critics' own
limited willingness to concede the Negro's humanity, as
evident in their denial of his spiritual and creative resources,
their interpretation of his experience as totally bleak and
negative, and their insistence that only Western contacts
provided him with the means of his uplift.   Thus, Nichols,
an American and onetime director of the America Institute
of the Free University of Berlin, misappropriating some of
the arguments in Richard Wright's "The Literature of the
Negro in the United States," describes the Afro-American
experience as producing "rage, guilt, ... self-disparage-
ment, ... and visionary hope"; only since Negro artists
have "apprenticed" themselves to Western culture, have
they been able to rise and transmute their negative experiences into art.   Black culture, folk as well as formal, is
impotent (jazz is "the cynic's flight into pure sensation ...
its voice ... like a hysterical cry for help even in its most
joyful ecstasy" (NSM, 1965, p. 125).

Similar attitudes are evident in other Marxist essays,
e.g., R. Orlowa, KL (1966), and Karl Heinz Wirzberger,
DAW (1967).   The former's argument, denying the Negro's
very self-knowledge, is an interesting echo of Werner Helwig's 1954 review of Unsichtbar (see pp. 96-97 above).
Black authors, Orlowa states, are only capable of articulating feelings of victimization and impotence (Ellison's essay
"Harlem is Nowhere" is cited in this connection); it takes a
white author to express the black experience to the fullest,
as will be attested by William Styron's forthcoming The Con-
fessions of Nat Turner.   Preposterous though this may seem,
the writer is totally in earnest.   Wirzberger's ponderous
analysis follows somewhat more familiar Marxist lines, but
his argument is equally predicated on the denial of black
autonomy, in this case of present-day black nationalism.
Taking Ellison as his text he deplores the dichotomy between
the great formal progress of contemporary Afro-American
literature and its thematic regression.   (The interested
reader may study this part of the argument in the more
easily accessible English critique of Ellison by Ernest
Kaiser, BlackW, 1970. )

Ellison's pioneering use of black idiom, Wirzberger
says, the suggestiveness of his invisibility symbol, his conscious search for appropriate modes of expression, have all
expanded the range of black literary tradition.   Thematically,
however, this literature has broken with its own progressive
tradition of the 1920's and 1930's, when it considered itself

as a weapon and collaborated in fighting the class conflict which is at the root of all racial conflict. Today's black American writers, with the possible exception of John Oliver Killens (a great favorite of German-speaking Marxist critics), [25] who may yet write the great American Negro novel, seem to move toward an unrealistic historically unpractical dead end, with their turn to individualism and sex (Brown and Baldwin), or to extreme separatism (Jones). Here again, Ellison's example is instructive, both in his choice of theme and in his dramatization of the unfortunate misunderstandings between black intellectuals and the American Communist Party. The Afro-American's claim to autonomous resources is thus clearly labeled a betrayal-- of himself as well as of the common cause of "progressive" black-white cooperation.

Though the almost blatant racism of the aforementioned studies is fairly widespread, one may also point to work in which the subject of race is not so prominent. The essays by Ursula Brumm, a particularly prolific scholar, are especially valuable. Her survey of the American novel from the 1930's to the present (JAS, 1964) is worth reading in conjunction with Wirzberger's similar study. In contrast to him, Brumm cites I. M. as evidence of her contention that the postwar fictional turn toward the individual represents progress, that it has enriched the literary tradition and social criticism as well. A number of her other studies, tracing the use of the Christ-Adam typology in American literature from Melville through Ellison, provide a novel context for reading the latter as part of that small group of writers set apart through their tragic sense of life.

In another thematic study entirely devoted to I. M., George Knox (Fabula, 1971) analyzes Ellison's ironic uses of the medieval dance-of-death motif.

Both Annette T. Rubinstein (SF, 1968) and Monika Plessner (Merkur, 1970) approach contemporary black literature as an intellectual documentary; the latter analyzes I. M.'s symbolism and its symbolic use of language as an index to Ellison's thought.

The single most useful essay, which is far more comprehensive than its title would indicate, is that of Heinz Rogge (NS, 1958). Broad, replete with information in its text and references, it provides the reader with

important biographical details and reveals close reading of
Ellison's prose writings; Rogge elucidates the conceptual
roots of I.M., notes highlights of its American reception,
wherein he gives a rarely found account of black critics as
well as white, and sums up with an Ellison-Wright comparison. Rogge's conclusions are fairly much in line with the
rest of German criticism, though much more thoroughly
presented and supported: Ellison's merit is that he has
given a new and original perspective to the American novel,
and that he has liberated himself from the proletarian
realism characterizing Afro-American literature hitherto.
Looking beyond the simple aim of integration, since skin
color is no guarantee of humanity, his chief aim is to explore the meaning of this humanity and the obstacles to its
attainment. He succeeds admirably in elucidating both the
drama of race relations and its paradigmatic character as
an American existential problem. Prophetically, Rogge also
suggests that future developments in race relations will de-
termine whether Afro-American literature will continue in
the wake of Ellison's thematic and plot development toward
the human in general, or whether it will turn away from
this direction. Fifteen years later, his question, only par-
tially answered, still stands, and his methodology offers a
fertile field for the serious study Ellison has not yet received in Germany.

## Notes

1.  "Was sie auch sonst trennen mag--gemein ist beiden
    das Suchen nach einem Weg aus der Verzweiflung
    und Hoffnungslosigkeit, die bisher so kennzeichnend
    für die junge Literatur war." (Zeit)

2.  John R. Frey, "America and her Literature Reviewed
    by Postwar Germany," JEGP, 20-21 (1953-1955), 5.

3.  See Franz H. Link, ed., Amerika: Vision und Wirk-
    lichkeit, Frankfurt/M.: Athenäum Verlag, 1968,
    and selected bibliography in the Appendix.

4.  William Faulkner: Essays, Speeches and Public Letters,
    ed. James B. Meriwether. New York: Random
    House, 1965, p. 120.

5.  "Aussergewöhnlicher Roman," Max Ruland, MM;
    "Grossartiger Roman," Günther Zacharias, Welt;

"... ein beinahe beängstigend gutes Stück Literatur
..., " Richard Kirn, <u>FNP</u>; "ein Wunderwerk in der
Verschränkung von Form und Thema, " rh, <u>Ge</u>; "eine
Leistung die innerhalb der Gipfelreihe amerikanischer
Erzählungskunst ihren Rang behauptet, " Werner Hel-
wig, <u>FAZ</u>.

6.   "The Art of Fiction: An Interview, " in <u>S & A</u>, p. 176.

7.   Axel Kaun, "Ein schwarzer Jedermann, " <u>BK</u>; Richard
     Kirn, "Roman der aüssersten Resignation, " <u>FNP</u>;
     Kurt Lenk, "Zum Optimismus verdammt, " <u>DStZ</u>.

8.   Wie glücklich dürfte die deutsche Literatur sein, wenn
     es gelänge, ein Buch--in den letzten Jahren gesch-
     rieben--zu finden, das auch nur annähernd so viel
     Phantasie mit rationalem Denken zu vereinen weiss.

9.   Über dem ganzen Roman liegt der Hauch des Märchens,
     trotz härtester Realistik, durch ihn zieht sich der
     Klang eines uralten Liedes hindurch, das uns allen
     gemeinsam, aber uns allen unbekannt und deshalb
     unaussprechbar ist.   Im literarkritischen Jargon
     sagt man dann wohl:   dieser Roman ist eine Dichtung.
     (<u>HA</u>)

10.  Die grausame, erregende Wirklichkeit entbehrt trotz
     ihrer Härte nicht der Güte des Humors und warmer
     Menschlichkeit.

11.  Man hat Amerika verherrlicht, und man hat es in
     Grund und Boden kritisiert.   Aber eine Stimme wie
     die Ellisons haben wir noch nicht gehört.   Sein
     Amerikabild ist bittersten Erfahrungen Stück um
     Stück abgerungen und in Licht und Schatten dennoch
     ausgewogen.   Literarisch menschlich und politisch
     ein Buch aus erster Hand.   (Günther Zacharias, <u>Welt</u>)

12.  Es bliebe abzuwarten, ob die ihm zuteil gewordene
     Auszeichnung eine Antwort, eine Bereitschaft auf diese
     Frage darstellte oder nur zu 'Nutzen neu aufgestellter
     innerpolitischer Programmpunkte rot angekreuzt wurde.

13.  ... niemals aber wurde der revolutionäre geistige
     Anspruch des Negers bisher mit solcher Deutlichkeit,
     Kraft und Tiefe dargestellt, wie in Ellisons Roman
     ... Was uns die schwarze Rasse zutragen könnte an

Kraft, an Dämonie, an Schärfung der Gewissen, kan
man aus Ellisons Buch erfahren. In diesem nicht
materiellen Sinne wird Amerika aufs neue zu einem
Kontinent der unbegrentzten Möglichkeiten. (StB)

14. Und das hat Ellison erreicht: scheinbar leidenschaft-
slos setzt er ein Bild neben das andere, zeichnet
realistisch in satten Farben, hütet sich vor jeder
billigen Sensation, ist in jedem Satz er selbst, und
malt in ungebrochener Kraft Situationen, die den
Leser in ihrer Einmaligkeit in Stoff und Form atem-
los machen. Dabei tastet er sich immer näher an
das Geheimnis Mensch heran, packt den Entgleiten-
den immer wieder neu und erfasst ihr zuletzt als
das Gegenteil eines Gottes, eines Heros, als zug-
leich gut und böse, als stark und schwach, als
schwarz und weiss. F. V., Mittag.

15. Ralph Ellison hat damit einen Weg beschritten, den
zwar Walt Whitman und später auch Thomas Wolfe
zu gehen versuchten. Aber es ist dennoch ein
neuer Weg, weil er von der Zeit immer wieder neu
vermessen wird. Es ist der dichterische Weg, das
eigene Land Sprache werden zu lassen. Der Erfolg
ist noch gering, aber er ist bereits ablesbar. Und
damit dürfte Ralph Ellison ... den Ruhm für sich
beanspruchen, mit seinem Roman Unsichtbar einen
Meilenstein in der amerikanischen Literaturgeschichte
gesetzt zu haben.

16. Wir sind die Unsichtbaren.... Er hat dem was wir
schon wussten, aber nicht zu benennen vermochten,
einen Namen gegeben.... Ein Neger kam und gab
uns unsern Namen. Wir müssen ihm danken. (HA)

17. Denn Ellisons mächtiger Roman ist, auf seinen seeli-
schen Kern zuruckgeführt, ein Dokument tiefster
Melancholie, um nicht zu sagen: künstlerisch ver-
brämter Verzweiflung und literarisch stilisierten
Ressentiments. Aus dieser wohl nur halb eingestan-
denen und deshalb um so zwiespältigeren Seelenlage
erklärt sich wahrscheinlich auch die geistige und
formale Zwiespaltigkeit des Buches ...

18. ... eine Pflanze mit weissen Blüten, doch schwarzen
Wurzeln. Ein Zwitter also ... In diesem Sinne
scheint mir Ralph Ellison ein erschütterndes

Beispiel intellektualistischer Verelendung zu geben.

19. Das Buch scheint ... zu bestätigen, dass der Neger
    zwar unser Sprach-und Kulturgewand anziehen, ja
    zu seiner "geistigen Haut" machen könne, ... dass
    ihm aber unsere Fähigkeit zum Verbalisieren der
    Spannungen fehlt.  Diese Fähigkeit ist nicht erlern-
    bar.

20. "... dieser grosse Dichter eines heutigen Neger-
    schicksals ..."

21. Der jetzt vierzigjährige Autor ist in einem Neger-
    internat erzogen worden.  Nicht lange dauerte für
    den Afrikaner, der er innerlich geblieben, das
    Erlernen europäisch-amerikanischer Weisheit....
    Von hier aus beginnt die Flucht: vor Europa, vor
    den Weissen, vor sich selbst--hinein in das Dasein
    "des Unsichtbaren," unter Verwerfung der gesamten
    Welt die ihn umgibt....  Die nachhaltigste Enttäus-
    chung wird ihn durch ... einer Bruderschaft ... der
    er beitritt, die ihn aber auf die Dauer nicht ertragen
    kann, wie er sie nicht erträgt, der allzu Erhliche,
    der mit allem Enthusiasmus zunächst Loslegende,
    der Gerade, der in einem gewichtigen Sinn Primitive
    und Naive.

22. In einer Zeit, da so viele Romane oberflächlich, glatt,
    gewandt, beschönigend und gespreizt oder form-
    und richtungslos sind, behandelt Unsichtbar mensch-
    liche Probleme, die kaum ein anderer Autor sah,
    und dies in einer Form und Spannweite von ungewöhn-
    licher Nachdenklichkeit, die in der Entwicklung lit-
    erarischer Kunst geradezu einen neuen Meilenstein
    setzt.

23. Publisher's Letter to compiler, dated June 29, 1971.

24. "Unsichtbar ist von der ersten bis zur letzten Seite
    eine Paraphrase auf Emersons berühmte Forderung
    nach einer allgemeinen Erziehung des Auges ..."

25. Another essay devoted to John Oliver Killens notes that
    Wright's, Ellison's and Baldwin's novels, which are
    so highly esteemed in "bourgeois" circles, reject
    the idea of family solidarity, and thereby, logically,
    also the solidarity of larger human groups, depicting

heroes who are devoid of human contacts or alien-
ated solitaries.   Horst Ihde, "Black Writer's Burden,
Bemerkungen zu John Oliver Killens, " <u>ZAA</u> 16
(1968),  117-137.

ITALY - ESSAYS

# INTRODUCTION

According to a 1970 survey, 77% of all Italian families possess no books at all, or fewer than ten. [1] Noteworthy Italian as well as foreign books are regularly brought to the public's attention by the Italian press--but the papers are read by only four out of ten adults, and purchased by only one out of ten. [2] Printed opinions on Ellison's work thus assume the nature of dramatic monologs, a fact which for better or worse ought to be kept in mind.

I. M. was reviewed in Italy, shortly after its American publication; Uomo invisibile, its Italian translation, was published in 1956, coinciding with Ellison's own stay in Rome during 1955-1957 as a Fellow of the American Academy of Arts and Letters, and received a respectable number of reviews. But there is little to indicate that the novel became popular with the general public or the academicians. Among the latter, Ellison appears to be somewhat grudgingly respected, but not studied; until very recently, in fact, Italian critics appeared insensitive to the issues which engage Ellison's attention, a fact which must be viewed in the context of a very lately acquired sensitivity toward American literature at large.

American translations head the list of foreign translations, but serious Italian study of American literature only began in the postwar years. Italians came to such study badly handicapped by physical lack of texts and, above all, by their own preconceptions: their inability to acknowledge America's cultural autonomy, to see its literature objectively rather than mythologize it, to confront it as art rather than sociology, and to divorce it from the fluctuations of popular pro- or anti-American feeling. Since World War II, much has been done toward "placing American studies in Italy on a more objective and less adventurous basis":[3] special American studies programs, a 1955 radio series on American literature directed by Salvatore Rosati and resulting in

his 1956 history, which was one of the first in this field;
publication, also since 1955, of Studi Americani, a journal
entirely devoted to American studies which undertook the
organization of systematic bibliographies.   The number of
Americanists has increased, and their essays appear with
greater frequency in newspapers such as Il Mondo and La
Fiera letteraria.

     As may well be imagined, the legitimizing of Amer-
ican literature did not simultaneously embrace its Afro
branch.   The subject is dismissed with a sentence or two in
literary histories of the 1950's (e. g., those by Carlo Izzo,
Rolando Anzilotti, Salvatore Rosati) and the 1960's (e. g.,
Sergio Perosa, 1965, and Alfreddo Rizzardi, 1963).   Be it
noted to the credit of Italian scholarship, however, that the
omission is lately being rectified apace, especially with respect to the organizing of available materials and study
tools.   The extensive Afro-American bibliography which appears in the 1971 issue of SA lists an extraordinary number
of authors available in Italian translations (some, like Zora
Neale Hurston, as early as 1946), with a decided prepon-
derance of poetry, separately and in collections.   But in
this field, as in that of "white" American literature, Italian
scholarship faced the difficult task of relinquishing preconceptions which had become articles of faith and were even
endowed with academic respectability by being promulgated
in special studies such as that of Claudio Gorlier in 1963;
to wit:   books about Negroes cannot project meaningful human experience; Afro-Americans basically operate within
a cultural vacuum; they have no viable folk tradition; no
formal tradition has as yet found its voice.   Hence, black
writers (especially fiction writers) labor under a crushing
inferiority complex, from which they are only now painfully
emerging.   The SA list of translations documents this attitude in the total absence of pre-Langston Hughes fiction
and prose.   Of all DuBois' writings, only the poem "A
Litany at Atlanta" is translated.

     The bulk of Italian writing on Ellison dates from the
1950's and early 1960's, and is hence marked by the aforementioned attitudes, and is not very illuminating.   But with
the new trend toward objective study of Afro-American literature and an understanding of its complexities, Italian
scholars may yet accomplish the feat of liberating Ellison
from their own past platitudes.

## I.  BIOGRAPHICAL INFORMATION


In spite of the fact that Ellison spent two years in
Italy as an American Academy of Arts Fellow, living in
Rome and lecturing in other cities during 1955-1957, very
little accurate biographical information is available about
him in Italian sources.

The prestigious Dizionario letterario Bompiani degli
autori di tutti i tempi e di tutti le letterature (1956, with
1964-66 supplements) ignores Ellison altogether.  The
Dizionario universale della letteratura contemporanea, III
(1960) includes him in its table of significant authors, but
the biographical entry is incomplete as well as erroneous in
its attribution of a Pulitzer prize to him.  (This alleged
Pulitzer prize, incidentally, is an almost ubiquitous Italian
contribution to misinformation about Ellison.)

Firsthand "portraits" and interviews are limited in
number.  An early interview conducted by Giuseppe Berto
during Ellison's stay in Italy is short on personal facts, but
potentially useful (no one seems to have read it), in elucidating major points about Uomo invisibile (hereafter, U. i.).
Another account of a meeting with Ellison, apparently at a
lecture he gave in Milan, appears several years later in
Fernanda Pivano's America rossa e nera (1964).  Here
impressionism runs rampant--"he looks at the world with
big melancholy eyes"[4]--attended by an exhaustive sartorial
inspection which averts its gaze only after reaching the
socks; the very ring on Ellison's finger gives off symbolic
emanations, becoming an Ariadne's thread to ensure his
safe return from the labyrinths of foreign travel.  A reviewer who found U. i. chaotic also unleashes his imagination in describing the author so as to reflect the alleged
characteristics of the book:  "Luxuriant, in full bloom like
an oak-tree, Ellison is full of sap, of pure blood, of a
vigor which is youthfully tumultuous and also excessive."[5]
Hard facts are difficult to come by under such manhandling.

The other available interview material originates in
New York.  A sympathetic "portrait" is drawn by Marisa
Bulgheroni for Mondo in 1960.  Also in that year, Bulgheroni's book, Il romanzo americano, includes a 1959 interview
in which questions of broad cultural import are explored.
A brief biographical note at the end of her book also offers
some general facts (while repeating the Pulitzer prize error).

The last word available up to the cutoff date for this
study appears in 1971, when the prestigious Corriere della
Sera prints a rather disappointing piece sent from New York
by Sergio Perosa.  As one might expect from the date, the
conversation deals with black militancy, cultural pluralism,
and the like; the interviewer finds Ellison rather pedantic,
and speculates on the possibility that his creative powers
may be burnt out.   Far from bringing to the interview a
foreign observer's more detached perspective, Mr. Perosa
seems instead to have absorbed and reflected most of the
superficial banalities on the subject that he found at hand in
America, thus contributing to further stereotyping of Ellison
rather than to information about him.


## II.   BIBLIOGRAPHIES


No work at all has been done in the primary and
very little in the secondary area.   Only the Dizionario
universale ... is aware of Ellison's short stories, listing
"Did You Ever Dream Lucky?"   All other sources list only
I. M., occasionally noting its Italian translation.

The reader searching for critical appraisals of Ellison was until the very late 1960's seriously handicapped
by lack of secondary bibliographies.   The pioneering bibliography of American literature, published by SA in its
1964 volume, lists only three Italian essays under Ellison.
The two very useful volumes of Repertorio bibliografico
della letteratura Americana in Italia only extend their
coverage to 1959 and, moreover, appeared with considerable delay, in 1966 and 1969 respectively.   Since the editors
included book reviews in their list, the 1969 volume is helpful in its partial listing of reviews of Uomo invisible which
appeared in 1956.

A special bibliography of Afro-American literature in
Italy appeared in the 1971 volume of SA, which came out
after a long delay, almost too late for use by this compiler.
In bringing together all available material, including survey
books, collections, translations and criticism, this bibliography performs an inestimable service.   It is, however,
difficult to use:  the criticism section, for example, consists of an alphabetical listing of critics, thus forcing the

reader to go through the whole list in order to extract from
the brief annotations those items pertaining to a specific
author. The same procedure applies for finding translations
such as short stories which are included in collections rather
than published separately. This makes consultation both
laborious and subject to error. In Ellison's case, very
little new material is added by this bibliography. It is,
however, of interest to note the impressive quantity of work
done in the field in general, as well as the variety of Afro-
American authors available in translation, ranging from
James Edwin Campbell to George Jackson, although fiction
is confined mostly to "moderns" such as Hughes, Wright,
Demby, Baldwin, Ellison.


## III.  PRINCIPAL REVIEWS


In 1953, three years before the appearance of I. M. 's
Italian translation, the novel was brought to the attention of
Italian readers by two reviews of its American edition.
Salvatore Rosati (Mondo, October 27, 1953) and Agostino
Lombardo (Sp, August, 1963), both respected Americanists,
judged the book an artistic failure, mostly because their
presumption about Negro writing would automatically pre-
clude any other judgment. His Negroness leads Ellison
into what both critics consider grotesque distortions of reality through violence, puppet-like characters and denunciatory passion. While Rosati attributes these weaknesses to a
persistent "racial inferiority complex, " Lombardo diagnoses
them as the inevitable recourse of the Negro writer's
"wounded soul" to the tradition of literary protest. Having
thus effectively neutralized Negro writing by attributing to
its practitioners the distorting lenses of anger and pain,
these critics, like many others, conveniently free themselves from the need to confront such writing as an authentic projection of reality. 6

Since he cannot share the enthusiasm of American
critics, Rosati can only account for the novel's extraordinary
American success by drawing upon some familiar stereotypes (see French reactions, pp. 65-66, 74 above):
Americans liked the book, he says, because of their peculiar taste for crudity--a taste which may in part be unconscious sadism, and which differs but little from the emotions

felt by spectators at the old Roman circus. [7]   His own reaction thus proclaims superior Old World breeding joined to
literary judgment (good grammar and good taste).

        Upon its publication in 1956, Uomo invisibile received
eighteen reviews.   Regrettably, a number of these were in-
accessible, so that the discussion that follows offers a partial rather than a representative picture.

        Ostensibly the Italian reviewers favor any departure
from the "narrow" protest tradition which has relegated
Negro literature to second- or third-rate status.   Yet their
reaction to U. i. suggests that they are unable to find alter-
nate criteria for judging Negro literature which is not protest.   The majority seem unprepared for such a book, ill
at ease, if not downright hostile.   As with Rosati, one reaction is the fastidious recoil in the name of good taste from
single scenes such as the Battle Royal ("one of the coarsest,
most perverted scenes one has ever read"[8]), or from the
whole book ("this deafening, bitter chaos of adventures and
sensations, "[9] "which leaves one most perplexed and ... dis-
mayed ... with so many conspiracies, crimes, acts and
speeches of an immoral vulgarity"[10]).   Seemingly hooked on
literal reading, these reviewers understandably find few re-
wards in U. i.   At best such an approach, so ill-suited to
this book, can yield only qualified approval, such as Piero
Mirizzi's (GM):  both as a documentary and as a literary
achievement the novel is of great interest, but its prolixity,
lack of balance, and above all, the author's subjectivity,
deny it supreme excellence.   Paolo Padovani (ICS) considers
the book a failure, because of the discontinuity of its parts
and the lack of a moral/political solution.   The book has
been touted as a contribution to the understanding of Afro-
Americans and of the human condition, complains the anonymous reviewer for the pro-Communist Paese Sera, yet most
of it is unintelligible.   Could it be, he snidely inquires,
that the machiavellian and simpleminded moral of the grandfather's words is what earned the novel so many prizes in
America?   Nor did the reviewers take the trouble to refer
to Ellison's own statements for an explanation of his aims.
Besides the National Book Award acceptance speech so
widely quoted in Germany, there was material closer to
hand in Giuseppe Berto's 1956 interview of Ellison, wherein
major points about U. i. are elucidated--regrettably, it would
seem, to an audience of one.   Unable or reluctant to acknowledge Ellison's experiment as a conscious exploration
of new narrative means, the reviewers retain the yardstick

of naturalism, interpreting his performance variously as an
antipathy for rational control, or as irrepressible racial
emotionalism wherein are reflected "not so much the truth
of the circumstances, as the outrages inflicted on the victim's soul...."11

In view of the fact that the distinguishing mark of
the Italian criticism perused appears to be a predilection
for rhetorical flights of fancy, and often for lack of intelli-
gibility, it is difficult to understand the strictures upon
Ellison on these grounds. Here, for example, is a sample
from the insights of one reviewer about Negro personality
and culture as gleaned from U.i. The reader will perhaps
agree that any relationship to the text is purely coincidental
here.

> ... his people ... impotent to free itself, in spite
> of its explosions of rage ... diligent and sad ...
> tenacious and faithful, enthusiastic and contradic-
> tory, fleeting and unfaithful, capable of suffering
> without winking an eye-lash, yet suddenly possessed
> by blind and bloody rage leading it to crime ...
> judicious and tempered, suddenly filled with beastly
> instincts, generous, impetuous, excessive in its
> reactions, charged with irrepressible vital convul-
> sions: that the author expresses and communicates
> all this to the reader, this much, it seems, can
> be agreed upon. 12

Fortunately, some exceptions to this supercilious
aridity can be cited. Like his colleagues, Bruno Fonzi
(Mondo) also reads U.i. as a sociological document and a
protest novel which operates within a Negro cultural vacuum.
But, unlike them, he feels that Ellison's original attempt to
represent the unconscious, irrational roots of racism thus
blending the inner with the outer world of experience, makes
major contributions to the creative potential of the protest
tradition. Two other reviewers, mirabile dictu, even dis-
card the documentary crutch, venturing into an independent
exploration of the book's variety. The following may serve
to sum up their reactions:

> To show the conscience of a nation within the con-
> science of an individual, to represent and syn-
> thesize a large, rich, fervid contrast, this was
> Ellison's aim, an aim which after reading one
> must conclude that he has carried out. Ellison

speaks like one of the true American classics
.... 13

Refreshing departures from the norm notwithstanding,
the perplexities of the majority of Italian reviewers seen
lead to the reluctant conclusion that 1956 was perhaps a
premature date for the publication of I. M. in Italy.


## IV.   CRITICAL STUDIES


Very few studies of Ellison are available, and, in
general, Italian scholarship presents the reader with numerous difficulties owing to its convoluted syntax, its wordiness,
its subjectivity.

The earliest critical essay available, is Glauco Cambon's discussion of I. M. in the March, 1953 issue of Aut
Aut.  In essence, Cambon's analysis of the novel stresses
its transcendence of the "race resentment" and the social
problems from which it draws its primary inspiration,
through Ellison's apt use of existentialism and symbolism.

Two other essays, by Salvatore Rosati (L'ombra dei
padri ..., 1958) and by Agostino Lombardo (Realismo e
simbolismo ..., 1957), are reprints of reviews published
in 1953 (see preceding section).  Rosati's minor alterations
sustain his earlier negative judgment which is qualified now
only by his concession of a possible dimension of psychological realism in the novel.  Lombardo's earlier criticism
is sustained and even strengthened by his 1961 context which
juxtaposes discussions of Ellison and Herbert Gold.  Though
Gold is also concerned with protesting specific historic in-
justices, Lombardo pronounces his work to be artistic, because his "whiteness" endows him with distancing abilities
which are denied to black writers such as Wright or Ellison.
(This myth transcends all national boundaries. )

Four years later, in the wake of studies by other
Americanists, Lombardo concedes a willingness to modify
his viewpoint, but the change is merely a swapping of critical clichés--Ellison, he says, is not mired in race, but is
indeed striving with very partial success to transcend race
in favor of the universal (La ricerca del vero, 1961, p. 364,
n. 7).

Marisa Bulgheroni's discussion of Ellison in the chapter on Negro fiction from her book Il nuovo romanzo americano, 1945-1959 (1960) credits the "unexpected metaphysical bounce" of I.M. with exerting a liberating influence on Negro literature, breaking its enslavement to sociology and its dilemma of Nationalism versus Assimilation. Bulgheroni carefully traces his early writing career and the fruitful influence exerted upon him by some tenets of the New Criticism: his exploration of folklore, of rhetorical depth and flexibility, of the American past and of symbolic history, allowed him to render experience which remains faithful to the specific black reality while incorporating it into the American context. In so doing he defined a new literary climate while also joining the ranks of the top writers of his country.

Claudio Gorlier's Storia dei negri degli Stati Uniti (1963) devotes space to a discussion of Ellison within his chapter on Negro narrative. In Gorlier's judgment, Ellison and Baldwin (the latter to a lesser extent) have brought the Negro novel to maturity. Ellison's maturity is defined as the overcoming of the Negro's permanent inferiority complex (see Rosati) and the broadening of his horizon beyond the color line. More perceptive than this summary of it implies, however, Gorlier's discussion takes full cognizance of the various components of Ellison's art: he recognizes its indigenous quality as rooted in both the Negro and the American traditions, while at the same time provinciality is evaded by reference to European culture. In effect, Gorlier considers the novel as an invigorating departure from the sterility of contemporary American letters. His essay marks various lines of approach which might have been fruitfully followed by other critics.

Six years separate Gorlier's work from the single other study of Ellison done subsequently, Bruno Cartosio's long essay in SA (1960). Here one finds evidence of the new trend toward objective study of Afro-American literature: copious documentation, frequent references to S & A and to several of Ellison's short stories, a more accurate conception of the role of folk culture in the novel, familiarity with the work of recent American scholarship. Having placed the novel in literary and political context, then analyzed it in its folk, thematic and symbolic components, Cartosio reaches the conclusion that Ellison's esthetic is limited and has been superseded by history. He notes Ellison's decreased productivity since 1952 as following naturally

upon the limitations imposed by an abstract affirmation of
values at a time of action; Ellison's growing inability to
order chaos, as evidenced especially in his piece "Tell It
Like It Is, Baby" (Nation, September 20, 1965), underlines
his remoteness from the former lucidity of his own invisible man, preparing to emerge from the underground and
act.    Although no black critics of Ellison are cited, Cartosio's argument clearly follows one line of black thinking
which brands Ellison as irrelevant and detached from the
struggle for liberation.    This essay, taken together with
the 1971 Perosa interview (see sec. I above), suggests that
time, by reintroducing the documentary approach, has vin-
dicated the Italian critics and given them additional reasons
for repudiating Ellison's work.

## V.   GENERAL ESTIMATES

        In view of the scarcity of work done on Ellison, the
frequent allusions to him--often as a reference point and
model of accomplishment in the twin fields of American and
black American literature--come as somewhat of a surprise.

        This status without study results from the reiteration
of a few unexamined though well-worn critical "insights."
Foremost is Ellison's purported "transcendence" of protest;
for an absurd rendition of this theme, see Dario Montalto
who lectures black writers on the necessity to liberate themselves from the black perspective, and in the very same
breath criticizes Ellison for weakening the force of his protest, and thereby "reducing" I. M. to a psychological novel
(Questioni, July-September. 1956).

        Other highlights of Ellison's reputation include his
concern for the individual in a mass society, and his preoccupation with the ethical function of the novel.    When
black literature is the context of discussion, comparisons
with Baldwin proliferate, with a fairly even division of
opinions as to the relative merits of each writer over the
other.    One interesting discussion suggests that Baldwin is
the culminating point of Afro-American literature, adding
that Ellison's "neurotic and unredeemable" protagonist has
been superseded by the work of younger writers such as
Charles Wright (Furio Colombo, Il Verri, 1964).

Along the fringes of academic criticism one even
hears strangely misplaced echoes of Black Arts rhetoric.
With brash self-confidence, Alessandro Portelli, one of the
younger critics, takes it upon himself to reject both Ellison
and Baldwin, on the grounds that as "Negro intellectuals"
they are incompetent to articulate the "authentic" black experience, which is the province of the folk. Claudio Gorlier's rejoinder (Approdo, March, 1970), pinpoints the fal-
lacies of Portelli's argument, but that the discussion itself
should arise in a milieu so far removed from firsthand
knowledge and study of the subject is an embarrassing example of white critical presumptuousness.


Notes

1.  PubW, 198 (December 7, 1970), 25. See also enquiry
    in FiL, no. 15, May 23, 1971, entitled "Perchè si
    legge poco" ("Why people read so little").

2.  The 40% reading statistic is from a 1958 survey with a
    1964 followup by John C. Merril et al., eds., The
    Foreign Press (Baton Rouge, Louisiana State Univer-
    sity Press, 1970), p. 103. The data on newspaper
    purchases appears in a NYT feature on the Italian
    press December 10, 1973, p. 20.

3.  Agostino Lombardo, "La critica italiana sulla lettera-
    tura americana," SA, 5 (1959), 9-49, an English
    summary of which is provided by the journal. Cf.
    also Tommaso Pisanti, "Il 'mito' della letteratura
    nordamericana in Italia," NA, 488 (July, 1963), 313-
    322; Alfredo Rizzardi, "America: realtà nella lette-
    ratura," FiL, 12, no. 42, October 20, 1957, p. 4,
    and Claudio Gorlier, "La nostra America," Approdo,
    16, no. 49 (March, 1970), 129-132.

4.  "Ora gira il mondo coi grandi occhi melanconici ..."
    (p. 242).

5.  Ridondante, rigoglioso come una quercia, Ellison e
    pieno di linfa, di sangue genuino, di vigore gio-
    vanilmente tumultuoso e, anche, disordinato. Ini-
    sero Cremaschi, GdP.

6.  Rosati's judgments about Negro writing have proved im-
    pervious to time. His second edition of Storia della

letteratura americana (1956, 1967), excludes black
authors from the American canon, with the exception
of one sentence on Wright whose "naturalism" and
"violence" are pronounced as products not of a literary school, but of a state of mind (p. 250).

7.   ... ma nessuno potrebbe persuaderci che nel successo
     non entrino anche, e in larga misura, la crudezza
     di certe scene che sembrano molto atte a stimolare
     un gusto acre diffuso tra i lettori americani....
     Insomma, una punta di crudeltà: certamente incon-
     scia, certamente espressione d'uno spirito romantico,
     più vivo, tra gli Americani, di quanto per solito si
     creda ma non poi tanto lontana dall'emozione degli
     antichi spettatori de giuochi circensi.

8.   "... una delle scene più crude e perverse che ci sia
     capitato di leggere." Renato Bertacchini, GdE.

9.   "... questo assordante, amaro caos di avventure e
     di sensazioni." Inisero Cremaschi, GdP.

10.  "... ci lascia molto perplessi e ... sgomenti ... con
     tante congiure, delitti, scene e discorsi d'una im-
     morale volgarità." Anon., CCa.

11.  "... riflettere cosi non tanto la verità delle circon-
     stanze, quanto gli oltraggi che esse infliggono all'-
     animo della vittima ..." Paolo Milano, Esp.

12.  ... del suo populo ... ancora impotente ad emanci-
     parsi, malgrado le sue esplosioni di colera ...
     laboriosa e triste ... tenace e fedele, appassionata
     e contraddittoria, sfuggente e infida, capace di sof-
     frire e di subire senza batter oglio e subitaneamente
     posseduta da un ira cieca e sanguinaria che l'induce
     al delitto, a momenti savia e temperante, a tratti
     dominata da instinti di fiera, generosa impetuosa
     smodata nelle sue reazioni, carica di fremiti vitali
     irreprimibili: che l'autore esprima e partecipi al
     lettore tutto questo, ci sembra si possa convenire.
     (Gianni Grana, FiL.)

13.  La coscienza d'una nazione nella coscienza d'un individuo,
     rappresentare in sintesi un grande, ricco, fervido
     contrasto, e stata la meta di Ellison, una meta, dob-
     biamo concludere, a lettura ultimata, raggiunta.

Ellison ci parla come i veri classici americani ...
O. D. B. ,  CN.   See also P. A. ,  Il Paese.

# SOME PENULTIMATE THOUGHTS

A familiar feature of medieval stories is the mysterious knight who appears uninvited before a noble assembly, challenging its heroes to some perilous adventure. By definition, it is in those days the mark of noble manhood to respond gladly to such hazardous offers, recognizing them as opportunities for the exercise and increase of chivalric virtue. Yet flesh and spirit often shrink from painful effort; if the challenge is particularly fearsome, the braves earnestly squirm and maneuver to escape from notice in the great hall.

It may, perhaps, not be too farfetched to use I. M. as a latter-day analogy to the redoubtable, always intrusive medieval challenger. In its twenty-year history this book has wandered far, always posing for its audiences challenges and opportunities such as would enhance our human growth; like its medieval predecessor, it too has encountered assiduous resistance, and much for the same reasons, although it has survived and thrived. Its challenges are intellectual of course, tailormade for a society which purportedly lives by ideas--provided these ideas do not perturb our individual/collective Weltanschauung. But I. M. invades the comfortable universe of detached literary analysis with a reading experience which, in the tradition of all authentic art, could involve us in profound personal change ("things as they are/Are changed upon the blue guitar"). As everyone knows, the reader is asked to come to terms with overwhelming sets of contraries--blackness and whiteness as interdependent aspects of each other, racism and American democracy, responsibility within anarchy, the one and the many, naturalism and fairy tale, sociology and myth, chaos and order. This is paradox of a vastly different order from the arid device we learn to cherish and chatter about in discussing modernist literature; we cannot cope with it meaningfully without the agon of remaking ourselves so as to accommodate its way of responding to the

124

world.   Hence a basic irony in the career of this very successful book, a "classic" to educated readers in America
and Europe, almost smothered in commentary, and yet
largely ignored on its most demanding and meaningful levels.
Since its 1952 publication in America, one or another dimension of its readers' makeup has consistently interposed
itself to short-circuit the book's total vision:   first it was
the white self-image, later the black; most recently it is
the renewed assault of sociology upon art which sets the
balance askew.   To be sure, any book, especially one like
I. M., must assert its worth within the context of our chaotic
everyday lives.   But the pressure of social and racial up-
heavals has created so much uncertainty that the tolerance
for broad reflection and inner change has all but disappeared
in the frenzied search of all parties for immediate, tangible
panaceas.   One misreads a novel if one seeks to extract
from it short-range social panaceas, and I. M. has certainly
been a dramatic casualty of such misreading.

     The question arose (and hence one reason for this
compilation) whether European scholarship, with its ad-
vantages of distance from the political and psychological
confrontations burdening white America, would offer less
resistance to involvement with Ellison's philosophy and art.
Such, on the whole, is not the case.   Non-homogeneous as
the European response is, it is nonetheless strongly marked
by a priori assumptions about the nature of black writing,
as well as about the nature of America, its literature and
culture, so that receptiveness is once again qualified.   And
lately Europe has been swept by the "documentary" fever
as much if not more than America, in the effort to comprehend present racial developments.

     I. M. 's European career offers one strange common
denominator:   even in countries like Germany which received
the novel most enthusiastically, its sensation invariably appears to exhaust itself in the reviews, generating no consistent scholarly spin-offs.   No work of particular bulk or consequence has been done in France, Germany or Italy, although Ellison enjoys unquestioned status in all three countries.   Similarly, no interest has developed (at least until
the end of 1971) in any of Ellison's other writings--hardly
anything besides I. M. has been translated into German,
French or Italian, nor has S & A, though the latter is
referred to.   In America, the opposite is of course true,
Ellison having become an increasingly fashionable subject
of academic essays and dissertations.   (By the end of 1971,

at a conservative and probably incomplete estimate, there
are 320 American items in the checklist as against a combined French, Italian, and German total of 163, among the
latter of which 50% constitutes reviews.) Yet anyone toiling
through this mass of American writing only emerges with
an impression of the vegetation all too often being choked
off by the undergrowth.

One rather unexpected finding of the present survey
is the minimal degree of scholarly interaction between the
European countries covered and America.  Faculty exchanges
are fairly frequent, and American scholarly work is found
in European translations; but on the whole, at least with
respect to Ellison, each of the countries seems to develop
its reactions independently and with minimal cross-reference.
This statement must be qualified with respect to the late
1960's, when Black Power rhetoric seems to have perco-
lated throughout Europe, especially so in France, finding
echoes in literary criticism.

Ellison's exposure to Europe follows shortly upon his
great American success:  French, German, and Italian
translations of I. M. appear within two years of each other,
the first two in 1954, the last in 1956.  Numerically,
Germany's response was the greatest, with Italy a poor
second, and France ignoring the book altogether except for
one review.  French interest only picked up in 1969, in
which year the novel was again coincidentally reissued in
both French and German; German interest remained high,
as evidenced by a large number of reviews.

The manner of each country's approach to Ellison is
quite distinct as well.  France has the largest quantity of
"personal" material, such as interviews and "portraits,"
even though, as far as is known, Ellison did not visit there
extensively as he did in Germany and especially Italy.  The
very few French critical studies are of high quality.  France
is also the only country among those studied whose government honored Ellison officially by bestowing upon him in
1968 its official Order of Arts and Letters, yet--paradox
again--the fact appears to be hardly known even in France.
Italy as of recently offers the best bibliographies and study
aids; it also has the earliest critical studies, beginning with
the 1950's, but these are generally of poor quality.  Germany has the most numerous as well as the most penetrating
reviews.

Varieties of white paternalism thrive in all three countries, though least so in Germany. In France the critical paternalism may be inferred by the neglect of the book until its 1969 reissue, when it was read primarily for its political content. In Italy, reviewer complaints about Ellison's subjective "distortion of American reality" are buttressed by repeated critical pronouncements about the Negro writers' long-standing "inferiority complex" and lack of cultural tradition. The rare but virulent German paternalism would deny the black writer even the capacity to articulate his own experience, adjudging white writers better equipped for the job. In none of these countries is consideration given to black scholarship, a trait shared with America, where the black perspective did not become heard until the middle and the late sixties.

The American reaction to the book, from more or less surprised and ignorant acclaim, through gradually deepening comprehension, from a totally white to an interracial experience of it, has been summarized in the introduction to that chapter. Of the European countries surveyed, only Germany might have served as a model for American critics in the early 1950's. At present, the European countries as a whole seem to lag behind America, because of their extreme politicizing of black literature. Undoubtedly I. M. in the long run did more for its readers at home than for those in Europe.

I. M. may not be a "great" book. But it is and will remain an important book, so long as the majority of us are unable to free ourselves from our habitual thought-categories, in order to respond to its comprehensive human vision.

UNITED STATES - CHECKLIST

## AMERICAN SECONDARY MATERIAL

### I. INTERVIEWS, "PORTRAITS," AND OTHER MISCELLANEOUS BIOGRAPHICAL

#### 1952-1964

1.  "Book Award Winner on CBS Radio." Los Angeles Sentinel, February 5, 1953, p. B-2.

2.  "Book Medals Won by M'Leish, Devoto." New York Times, January 28, 1953, p. 25.

3.  Breit, Harvey. "Talk with Ralph Ellison." New York Times Book Review, May 4, 1952, p. 26. Reprinted in The Writer Observed. New York: World Publishing Company, 1956, pp. 243-245.

4.  Cerf, Bennett. "Trade Winds." Saturday Review, 36 (February 7, 1953), 7.

5.  Chester, Alfred, and Vilma Howard. "The Art of Fiction: An Interview." Paris Review, no. 8 (Spring, 1955), 54. 71. Reprinted in George Plimpton, ed. Writers at Work. Second Series. New York: Viking Press, 1963, pp. 316-334. Reprinted in Shadow and Act. New York: Random House, 1964, pp. 167-183.

6.  Citation: Honorary Degree of Doctor of Humane Letters Awarded to Ralph Waldo Ellison. Tuskegee Institute, Alabama, April 7, 1963.

7.  Dempsey, David. "In and Out of Books." New York Times Book Review, February 1, 1953, p. 8. On National Book Awards.

8.  "Ellison, DeVoto, MacLeish Win National Book Awards." Publisher's Weekly, 163 (January 31, 1953), 531.

9.    "Ellison, MacLeish and DeVoto Win National Book
      Awards." Publisher's Weekly, 163 (February 7,
      1953), 744-746.

10.   "Ellison's 'Invisible Man' Wins Him Literary 'Oscar'."
      Pittsburgh Courier, national edition, February 7,
      1953, p. 5.

11.   "14 Join National Arts Institute: American Academy
      Inducts." New York Times, May 21, 1964, p. 41.

12.   "14 Members Elected to Arts Honor Unit." New York
      Times, February 18, 1964, p. 37.

13.   Geller, Allen. "An Interview With Ralph Ellison."
      Tamarack Review, no. 32 (Summer, 1964), 3-24.

14.   Girson, Rochelle. "Sidelights on Invisibility." Satur-
      day Review, 36 (March 14, 1953), 20+.

15.   Hazard, Eloise P. "Portrait." Saturday Review, 35
      (April 12, 1952), 23.

16.   "Ike Joins Press in Marking Newspaper Week." Vir-
      ginia Journal and Guide, March 21, 1953, p. 2.
      In connection with Russwurm Award.

17.   Martin, Gertrude. The Chicago Defender, April 5,
      1952, p. 11. Announcement of forthcoming pub-
      lication of Invisible Man.

18.   _____. The Chicago Defender, February 7, 1953,
      p. 11. On National Book Award.

19.   "National Book Awards." Nation, 176 (February 7,
      1953), 111.

20.   "National Book Awards." New York Times, January
      31, 1953, p. 14.

21.   Negro History Bulletin, 17 (October, 1953), 20.

22.   "Negro Press Gets Eisenhower Praise." New York
      Times, March 15, 1953, p. 58. In connection
      with Russwurm Award.

23.   "Newspaper Week Opens March 14." Amsterdam News,

March 14, 1953, p. 2. In connection with Russwurm Award.

24. "Newspaper Week Opens With Salute." The Chicago
Defender, March 21, 1953, pp. 1-2. In connection with Russwurm Award.

25. Parks, Gordon. "A Man Becomes Invisible: Invisible
Man translated into Pictures by Gordon Parks with
help from Ellison." Life, 33 (August 25, 1952),
9-11.

26. "Ralph Ellison Fiction Winner." Crisis, 60 (March,
1953), 154-156.

27. "Ralph Ellison on Radio Panel." Baltimore Afro-
American, February 7, 1953, p. 7.

28. "Ralph Ellison Wins National Book Award." Baltimore
Afro-American, February 7, 1953, p. 2.

29. "Ralph Ellison Wins National Book Award." Negro
History Bulletin, 16 (May, 1953), 183.

30. Samstag, N. A. and Ted Cohen. "An Interview with
Ralph Ellison." Phoenix (Fall, 1961), 4-10.
Literary magazine of the University of Chicago.

31. Stern, Richard G. "That Same Pain, That Same
Pleasure: an Interview." December, 3 (Winter,
1961), 30-32+. Reprinted in Shadow and Act,
pp. 23-41. Reprinted in A. Chapman, ed. Black
Voices. New York: New American Library, 1968,
pp. 645-659.

32. "Ten Get Russwurm Awards." Los Angeles Sentinel,
March 19, 1953, pp. 1+.

33. "Two Arts Groups Make 24 Awards." New York Times,
May 24, 1956, p. 25. Renewal of National Acad-
emy of Arts and Letters Fellowship Award to
Ellison.

34. "Visible Man." Newsweek, 62 (August 12, 1963), 81-
82.

35. "Winners and Friends." New York Times Book Review,

February 8, 1953, p. 25.   Pictures of National
Book Award winners.

## 1965-1971

36.  "A Bipartisan Group Sets Up Committee to Back
     Humphrey." New York Times, May 12, 1968,
     p. 56.

37.  "Citizen Unit to Aid Public TV System." New York
     Times, May 26, 1967, p. 94.

38.  "City Museum Adds Trustees to Board." New York
     Times, December 27, 1970, p. 50.

39.  Contemporary Authors, Vols. 11-12.  Detroit:  Gale
     Research Co., 1965.

40.  Corry, John.  "An American Novelist Who Sometimes
     Teaches." New York Times Magazine, November
     20, 1966, pp. 55ff.  Reprinted in special Ralph
     Ellison number of Black World, 20, no. 2 (Decem-
     ber, 1970), 116-125, under the title "A White
     View of Ralph Ellison."

41.  Current Biography Yearbook.  New York:  The H. W.
     Wilson Co., 1968.

42.  Ellison, Ralph.  "A Dialogue With His Audience."
     Barat Review, 3 (January, 1968), 51-53.

43.  Ellison, Ralph and James A. McPherson.  "Indivisible
     Man." The Atlantic, 226, no. 6 (December,
     1970), 45-60.

44.  Ellison, Ralph, William Styron, Robert Penn Warren,
     and C. Van Woodward.  "The Uses of History in
     Fiction." Southern Literary Journal, 1, no. 2
     (Spring, 1969), 57-90.

45.  "Festival in Senegal Honors Armstrong." New York
     Times, April 9, 1966, p. 12.

46.  "Ford Chooses Panel to Award Grants." New York
     Times, May 15, 1968, p. 95.

47.  International Library of Negro Life and History.
        Washington:  Associated Publishers, 1967-69.

48.  "Johnson Gives Freedom Medals to 20 for Meritorious
        Service."  New York Times, January 21, 1969,
        p. 29.

49.  "Johnson Sums Up:  He Has Helped the People."
        New York Times, January 14, 1969, pp. 1ff.

50.  Kostelanetz, Richard.  "Ralph Ellison:  Novelist As
        Brown-Skinned Aristocrat."  Shenandoah, 20,
        no. 4 (Summer, 1969), 56-77.  Reprinted in
        Kostelanetz' Master Minds:  Portraits of Con-
        temporary Artists and Intellectuals.  New York:
        Macmillan, 1969, pp. 36-59.

51.  "Life in Harlem:  View from the Back Street."  New
        York Times, September 4, 1966, sec. IV, p. 5.

52.  McGrady, Mike.  "Found:  A Nonprotester."  Newsday,
        October 28, 1967, pp. 3Wff.

53.  Negro Almanac.  Harry A. Ploski and Roscoe C.
        Brown, eds.  New York:  Bellwether, 1967.

54.  "New School Names Author."  New York Times, No-
        vember 10, 1968, p. 48.

55.  "Officers Elected by Arts Institute."  New York Times,
        February 2, 1967, p. 28.

56.  "1.8 Million Given By Arts Council."  New York Times,
        August 30, 1966, pp. 1ff.

57.  "Ralph Ellison is Chosen as Trustee of Channel 13."
        New York Times, May 7, 1968, p. 95.

58.  "Schweitzer Chair at N.Y.U. Goes to Ralph Ellison."
        New York Times, October 11, 1970, p. 56.

59.  "Senators Hear a Negro Praise Harlem."  New York
        Times, August 31, 1966, p. 32.

60.  Thompson, James, Lennox Raphael and Steve Cannon.
        "A Very Stern Discipline:  An Interview."  Harper's
        Magazine, 234, no. 1402 (March, 1967), 76-95.

136                                    The Blinking Eye

61.   Toppin, Edgar A.  A Biographical History of Blacks
      in America Since 1528.  New York:  McKay,
      1971, pp. 292-293.

62.   "Unit Named to Plan 200th Anniversary of U.S. Revo-
      lution."  New York Times, January 19, 1967,
      p. 40.

63.   Warren, Robert Penn and Ralph Ellison.  "A Dialogue."
      The Reporter, 32, no. 6 (March 25, 1965), 42-
      48.  Excerpts from Warren's Who Speaks for the
      Negro? (see following entry).

64.   Warren, Robert Penn.  Who Speaks For the Negro?
      New York:  Random House, 1965, pp. 325-354.
      Excerpted in The Reporter (see preceding entry).

65.   "Writers Appeal for Soviet Jews."  New York Times,
      August 3, 1969, p. 6.

66.   "Writers Appeal on Soviet Jews."  New York Times,
      May 21, 1967, p. 12.


                    II.  BIBLIOGRAPHIES


                 A.  Primary, 1952-1964

None.


                 B.  Primary, 1965-1971

67.   Benoit, Bernard and Michel Fabre.  "A Bibliography
      of Ralph Ellison's Published Works."  Studies in
      Black Literature, 2, no. 3 (Autumn, 1971), 25-28.

68.   Emanuel, James A., and Theodore L. Gross, eds.
      Dark Symphony.  New York:  The Free Press,
      1968, pp. 586-587.

69.   Lillard, R. Stewart.  "A Ralph Waldo Ellison Bibli-
      ography (1914-1967)."  The American Book Col-
      lector, 19 (November, 1968), 18-22.

70.  Moorer, Frank E., and Lugene Baily. "A Selected
     Check List of Materials By and About Ralph Elli-
     son. " Black World, 20 (December, 1970), 126-
     127.

71.  Polsgrove, Carol. "Addenda to 'A Ralph Waldo Elli-
     son Bibliography' 1914-1968. " The American
     Book Collector, 20 (November-December, 1969),
     11-12.


                  C.   Secondary, 1952-1964

72.  Gerstenberger, Donna L. and George Hendrick, comps.
     The American Novel 1789-1959: A Checklist of
     Twentieth Century Criticism.   Denver:   Alan
     Swallow, 1961, pp. 67-68.

73.  Nyren, Dorothy, comp.  A Library of American Criti-
     cism:  Modern American Literature, 3rd ed.
     New York:  Frederick Ungar Publishing Company,
     1964, pp. 163-164.


                  D.   Secondary, 1965-1971

74.  Combs, Richard E.  Authors:  Critical and Biographi-
     cal References.   Metuchen, N. J.:  The Scarecrow
     Press, 1971, p. 52.

75.  Emanuel, James A., and Theodore L. Gross, eds.
     Dark Symphony.  New York:  The Free Press,
     1968, pp. 587-588.

76.  Gerstenberger, Donna L., and George Hendrick, comps.
     The American Novel:  a Checklist of Twentieth
     Century Criticism on Novels Written Since 1789.
     Vol. II:  Criticism Written 1960-1968.  Chicago:
     The Swallow Press, Inc., 1970, pp. 80-82.

77.  Gibson, Donald B., ed.  Five Black Writers.  New
     York:  New York University Press, 1970, pp. 305-
     306.

78.  Gross, Seymour L., and John E. Hardy, eds.  Images
     of the Negro in American Literature.  Chicago:
     University of Chicago Press, 1966, p. 305.

138                                    The Blinking Eye

79.   Leary, Lewis, ed.  Articles on American Literature
      1950-1967.  Durham, North Carolina:  Duke Uni-
      versity Press, 1970, pp. 146-147.

80.   McCowell, Robert E., and George Fortenberry.  "A
      Checklist of Books and Essays About American
      Negro Novelists."  Studies in the Novel, 3, no. 2
      (Summer, 1971), 219-236.  Ellison entry, 229-231.

81.   Moorer, Frank E., and Lugene Baily.  "A Selected
      Check List of Materials By and About Ralph Elli-
      son."  Black World, 20 (December, 1970), 127-
      130.

82.   Reilly, John M.  Twentieth Century Interpretations of
      'Invisible Man':  A Collection of Critical Essays.
      Englewood Cliffs:  Prentice-Hall, 1970, pp. 119-
      120.

83.   Tischler, Nancy M.  "Ralph Ellison (1914-  )."  Louis
      D. Rubin, Jr., ed.  A Bibliographical Guide to
      the Study of Southern Literature.  Baton Rouge,
      Louisiana:  Louisiana State University Press, 1969,
      pp. 191-192.

84.   Turner, Darwin T., comp.  Afro-American Writers.
      New York:  Appleton-Century Crofts, 1970, pp. 52-
      53, 112.


            III.  SPECIAL ELLISON MATERIALS


Journals, collections, guides

85.   CLA Journal, 13, no. 3 (March, 1970).  Special
      Ralph Ellison number.

86.   Gottesman, Ronald.  Studies in Invisible Man.  Charles
      E. Merrill Studies.  Columbus, Ohio.  Charles
      E. Merrill Pub. Co., 1971.

87.   Phillips, Elizabeth C.  Ralph Ellison's Invisible Man.
      Monarch Notes.  New York:  Monarch Press, 1971.

88.   "Ralph Ellison:  His Literary Works and Status. "
      Black World, 20, no. 2 (December, 1970).  Spe-
      cial Ralph Ellison number.

89.   Reilly, John M. , comp.  Twentieth Century Interpreta-
      tions of Invisible Man.  Englewood Cliffs, N. J. :
      Prentice-Hall, 1970.

Tapes, film

90.   Ralph Ellison Interview With Warren Bower of WYNC,
      April, 1952.  Cassette tape; donated by Mr. Bower
      to Livingstone College, Salisbury, N. C.

91.   Ralph Ellison Talking With Studs Terkel of WFMT.
      January 17, 1963.  Mono tape.

92.   Turner, Darwin T.  Invisible Man.  Phonotape lec-
      ture.  Deland, Fla. :  Everett Edwards, 1970.

93.   U. S. A. :  The Novel--Ralph Ellison on Work in Pro-
      gress.  Film, produced, written and directed by
      Robert Hughes; filmed in Ellison's apartment.
      National Educational Television, 1966.

IV.   REVIEWS

A.   Invisible Man

94.   Barrett, William.  "Black and Blue: a Negro Céline. "
      American Mercury, 74 (June, 1952), 100-104.

95.   Bellow, Saul.  "Man Underground. "  Commentary, 13
      (June, 1952), 608-610.

96.   Berry, Abner W.  "Ralph Ellison's Novel 'Invisible
      Man' Shows Snobbery, Contempt for Negro Peo-
      ple. "  The Worker, June 1, 1952, sec. 2, p. 7.

97.   "Black and Blue. "  Time, 59 (April 14, 1952), 112.

98.   Booklist, 48 (July 15, 1952), 378.

99.  Brown, Lloyd L.  "The Deep Pit."  Masses and
     Mainstream, 5 (June, 1952), 62-64.  Reprinted in
     Reilly, pp. 97-99.

100.  Butcher, Margaret Just.  See Locke, Alain.

101.  Byam, Milton S.  "Invisible Man."  Library Journal,
      77 (April 15, 1952), 716-717.

102.  Cartwright, Marguerite D.  "S. P. D. N. M."  Amster-
      dam News, March 7, 1953, p. 14.

103.  _____.  "The Neurotic Negro."  Amsterdam News,
      March 14, 1953, p. 16.  Reprinted together with
      "S. P. D. N. M." in abbreviated form as a letter to
      the editor:  "Descendants of Bigger Thomas,"
      Phylon, 14, no. 1 (March, 1953), 116-118.

104.  Cassidy, T. E.  "A Brother Betrayed."  The Com-
      monweal, 56 (May 2, 1952), 99-100.

105.  Chase, Richard.  "A Novel Is a Novel."  Kenyon
      Review, 14, no. 4 (Autumn, 1952), 678-684.

106.  Curtis, Constance.  "Letter to the Editor."  Amster-
      dam News, March 14, 1953, p. 16.  Comments
      on Cartwright's article in defense of Ellison.

107.  Daiches, David.  "Writers' Shop Talk."  Saturday
      Review, 40 (November 16, 1957), 19-20.

108.  Hedden, Worth T.  "Objectively Vivid, Introspectively
      Sincere."  New York Herald Tribune Book Review,
      April 13, 1952, p. 5.

109.  Howe, Irving.  "A Negro in America."  Nation, 174
      (May 10, 1952), 454.

110.  Hughes, Langston.  "Langston Hughes."  Column in
      New York Age, February 28, 1953, p. 12.

111.  "Invisible Man."  Kirkus, 20 (February 1, 1952), 94.

112.  Kazin, Alfred.  Contemporaries.  Boston:  Little,
      Brown, 1962, pp. 212, 388.

113.  Killens, John O.  "Invisible Man."  Freedom (June,
      1952), 7.

114.  Langbaum, Robert.  Furioso, 7,  no.  4 (1952),  58.
      Carleton College,  Northfield,  Massachusetts.

115.  Lewis,  Richard W. B.  "Eccentrics' Pilgrimage."
      Hudson Review,  6,  no.  1 (Spring,  1953),  114-150.

116.  Locke,  Alain.  "From Native Son to Invisible Man:
      A Review of the Literature of the Negro for 1952."
      Phylon,  14,  no.  1 (March,  1953),  34-44.  A
      shorter version,  minus criticism of Ellison's
      verbosity is found in Butcher, Margaret J.,  The
      Negro in American Culture.  New York:  Knopf,
      1956,  pp.  179-180.

117.  Martin,  Gertrude.  The Chicago Defender,  April 19,
      1952,  p.  11.

118.  Mayberry,  George.  "Underground Notes."  New Re-
      public,  126 (April 21,  1952),  19.

119.  Morris,  Wright.  "The World Below."  New York
      Times Book Review,  April 13,  1952,  p.  5.

120.  Murray,  Florence.  "Letter to the Editor."  Amster-
      dam News,  March 28,  1953.  In defense of Mar-
      guerite D.  Cartwright's article (see above).

121.  Ottley,  Roi.  "Blazing Novel Relates a Negro's Frus-
      trations."  Chicago Sunday Tribune,  May 11,  1952,
      p.  4.

122.  Prattis,  P. L.  "The Horizon."  Column in the Pitts-
      burgh Courier,  April 4,  1953,  p.  7.

123.  Prescott,  Orville.  New York Times,  April 16,  1952,
      p.  25.

124.  Redding,  Saunders.  "Invisible Man."  Baltimore
      Afro-American,  May 10,  1952,  Afro-Magazine
      Section,  p.  10.

125.  Rolo,  Charles J.  "Candide in Harlem."  Atlantic,
      190 (July,  1952),  84.

126.  Schwartz,  Delmore.  "Fiction Chronicle:  The Wrongs
      of Innocence and Experience."  Partisan Review,
      19 (May-June,  1952),  354-359.

142                                      The Blinking Eye

127.  Smith, Lucymae.  New York Age, April 26, 1952,
      pp. 8+.

128.  "The Sustaining Stream."  Time, 81 (February 1,
      1963), 84.

129.  Webster, Harvey C.  "Inside a Dark Shell."  Satur-
      day Review, 35 (April 12, 1952), 22-23.

130.  West, Anthony.  "Black Man's Burden."  New Yorker,
      28 (May 31, 1952), 93-96.  Reprinted, with slight
      modifications, in West's Principles and Persuasions.
      New York:  Harcourt, Brace, 1957, pp. 212-218.
      Reprinted in Reilly, pp. 102-105.

131.  W. H. B.  "Among the New Books:  The Invisible Man."
      San Francisco Chronicle, July 27, 1952, p. 12.

132.  Winslow, Henry F.  "Unending Trial."  Crisis, 59
      (June-July, 1952), 397-398.

133.  Yaffe, James.  "Outstanding Novels."  Yale Review,
      n. s. 41, no. 8 (Summer, 1952), viii.


                     B.  Shadow and Act

134.  Abrahams, Roger D.  "Book Reviews."  Journal of
      American Folklore, 79 (1966), 493-494.

135.  Anon.  Choice:  Books for the College Library, 2,
      no. 1 (March, 1965), 16.

136.  Chevigny, Bell G.  Village Voice (November 19,
      1964), pp. 15+.

137.  Chisolm, Lawrence W.  "Signifying Everything."
      Yale Review, 54, no. 3 (Spring, 1965), 450-454.

138.  De Lissovoy, Peter.  "The Visible Ellison."  Nation,
      199 (November 9, 1964), 334-336.

139.  Elliott, George P.  "Portrait of a Man on His Own."
      New York Times Book Review, October 25, 1964,
      pp. 4-5+.

140.  Fuller, Hoyt.  "Books Noted."  Negro Digest, 14, no.
      10 (August, 1965), 51-52.

141. Hicks, Granville. "Prose and the Politics of Protest." Saturday Review, 47 (October 24, 1964), 59-60.

142. Hyman, Stanley Edgar. "Ralph Ellison In Our Time." Standards: a Chronicle of Books for Our Time. New York: Horizon Press, 1966, pp. 249-253.

143. "I Do!" Newsweek, 64 (October 26, 1964), 119-121A.

144. Jackson, Miles M. "Significant Belles Lettres By and About Negroes Published in 1964." Phylon, 26, no. 3 (Fall, 1965), 226-227.

145. Janeway, Elizabeth. "Anger is Just Not Enough." Christian Science Monitor, December 24, 1964, p. 5.

146. Janowitz, Morris. American Journal of Sociology, 70 (May, 1965), 732-734.

147. Kostelanetz, Richard. "Books: Critics' Choices for Christmas: Shadow and Act." The Commonweal, 83, no. 9, December 3, 1965, 285.

148. _____. "Ellison's Essays." Sewanee Review, 73, no. 1 (January-March, 1965), 171-172.

149. L. F[leischer]. "Forecast of Paperbacks: Nonfiction." Publishers' Weekly, 189, no. 26, June 27, 1966, 105.

150. Lewis, Richard W. B. "Ellison's Essays." New York Review of Books (January 28, 1965), 19-20.

151. Podhoretz, Norman. "The Melting-Pot Blues." New York Herald Tribune Book Week, October 25, 1964, pp. 1+.

152. Sale, Roger. "The Career of Ralph Ellison." Hudson Review, 18, no. 1 (Spring, 1965), 124-128.

153. "Shadow and Act." Library Journal, 89 (September 15, 1964), 153. Young adults section.

154. Van Benthuysen, Robert. "Shadow and Act." Library Journal, 89 (October 15, 1964), 3968.

155. Velde, Paul. "Shadow and Act." The Commonweal, 81 (February 19, 1965), 674-676.

156. Warren, Robert Penn. "The Unity of Experience." Commentary, 39 (May, 1965), 91-96.

157. Whittemore, Reed. "Beating that Boy Again." New Republic 151 (November 14, 1964), 25-26.


V.   GENERAL ESTIMATES


(Lists important critical assessments within discussions of which Ellison is not the primary subject.   Where relevant, items mentioned in the discussion appear in section VI, Critical Studies, also.)

1952-1964

158. Breit, Harvey. "James Baldwin and Two Footnotes." Nona Balakian and Charles Simmons, eds.  The Creative Present.  New York: Doubleday, 1963, pp. 1-23.

159. Cowley, Malcolm. The Literary Situation.  New York: Viking Press, 1954, pp. 4, 91ff.

160. Eisinger, Chester E.  Fiction of the Forties.  Chicago:  The University of Chicago Press, 1963, pp. 14, 70-71, 370ff.

161. Fiedler, Leslie A.  Love and Death in the American Novel.  New York:  Criterion Books, 1960, pp. 470-471.

162. _____.  Waiting for the End.  New York:  Stein and Day, 1964, pp. 104-108.

163. Geismar, Maxwell. "The Postwar Generation in Arts and Letters." Saturday Review, 36 (March 14, 1953), 11-12+.  Reprinted, with slight modification, in Geismar's American Moderns:  From Rebellion to Conformity.  New York:  Hill and Wang, 1958, pp. 15-19.

164. Hoffman, Frederick J. The Modern Novel in America. Rev. ed. Chicago: Henry Regnery Company, 1963, pp. xiv, 246, 248, 254.

165. Hughes, Carl Milton [Pseud.]. The Negro Novelist: A Discussion of the Writings of American Negro Novelists 1940-1950. New York: The Citadel Press, 1953, pp. 272-273.

166. Kazin, Alfred. "The Alone Generation." Harper's, 219, no. 1313 (October, 1959), 127-131. Reprinted in Kazin's Contemporaries. Boston: Little, Brown, 1962, pp. 207-217.

167. Krim, Seymour. "The Fiction of Fiction: A Critical Nudger." Partisan Review, 19, no. 3 (May-June, 1952), 351-353.

168. Lewis, Richard W. B. The American Adam. Chicago: University of Chicago Press, 1955, pp. 199, 200.

169. _____. "American Letters: A Projection." Yale Review, 51, no. 2 (December, 1961), 211-226.

170. Ludwig, Jack B. Recent American Novelists. University of Minnesota Pamphlets on American Writers, no. 22. Minneapolis: University of Minnesota Press, 1962, pp. 18-24.

171. Mailer, Norman. Advertisements For Myself. New York: G. P. Putnam's Sons, 1959, p. 471.

172. Roth, Philip. "Writing American Fiction." Commentary, 31, no. 3 (March, 1961), 223-233. Reprinted in The American Novel Since World War II, Marcus Klein, ed. New York: Fawcett, 1969, pp. 142-158.

173. "Tell It Like It Is." Newsweek, 64 (August 24, 1964), 84-85.

174. Thorp, Willard. American Writing in the Twentieth Century. Cambridge, Mass.: Harvard University Press, 1960, pp. 134+.

1965-1971

175.  "American Fiction:  the Postwar Years, 1945-1965."
      New York Herald Tribune Book Week, September
      26, 1965, pp. 1ff.

176.  "Black Writers' Views on Literary Lions and Values."
      Negro Digest, 17, no. 3 (January, 1968), 10-48,
      81ff.

177.  Cruse, Harold.  The Crisis of the Negro Intellectual.
      New York:  William Morrow, 1967, pp. 505-511
      and elsewhere.

178.  Dupee, F. W.  "On Invisible Man."  New York
      Herald Tribune Book Week, September 26, 1965,
      pp. 4, 26-27.

179.  Gayle, Addison, Jr.  "The Critic, the University, and
      the Negro Writer."  Negro Digest, 16, no. 3
      (January, 1967), 54-58.

180.  _____.  "The Function of Black Literature at the
      Present Time."  In The Black Aesthetic, Gayle
      Addison, Jr., ed.  New York:  Doubleday & Co.,
      Inc., 1972, pp. 383-394.  Essay originally writ-
      ten in 1970.

181.  Hagopian, John V.  "Mau-Mauing the Literary Estab-
      lishment."  Studies in the Novel, 3, no. 2 (Sum-
      mer, 1971), 135-147.

182.  Henderson, Stephen E.  "Survival Motion:  a Study
      of the Black Writer and the Black Revolution in
      America."  In The Militant Black Writer, Mercer
      Cook and Stephen E. Henderson, eds.  Madison,
      Wisconsin:  University of Wisconsin Press, 1969,
      pp. 65-129.  Ellison portion, pp. 95-99 et seq.

183.  Igi, Eka.  "Note From a Non-Intellectual on Ralph
      Ellison."  ("Commemorating the Non-Completion
      of his Second Novel.")  Black World, 20, no. 6
      (April, 1971), 97.  Satiric poem.

184.  Jeffers, Lance.  "The Death of the Defensive Posture:
      Toward Grandeur in Afro-American Letters."  The
      Black 70's, Floyd B. Barbour, ed.  Boston:

Porter-Sargent, 1970, pp. 253-263. Ellison portion, pp. 260-262.

185. Johnson, Alicia L. "Fish (* = Spirit (For Ralph Ellison)." Black World, 20, no. 2 (December 1970), 115. Poem.

186. Kaiser, Ernest. "Negro Images in American Writing." Freedomways, 7, no. 2 (Spring, 1967), 152-163. The brief but caustic portion pertaining to Ellison is reprinted in John M. Reilly, ed. Twentieth Century Interpretations of Invisible Man, p. 111. [See no. 82]

187. Kostelanetz, Richard. "The Negro Genius." Twentieth Century, 175, no. 1033 (Second Quarter, 1967), 49-50. British Journal.

188. Mason, Clifford. "Black Fiction: a Second Look." Life, 68, no. 17 (May 8, 1970), 18.

189. "Ralph Ellison and the Establishment." Negro Digest, 16, no. 10 (August, 1967), 49-50.

190. Redding, Saunders. "Since Richard Wright." African Forum, 1, no. 4 (Spring, 1966), 21-31.

191. Williams, John A. "Ralph Ellison and Invisible Man: Their Place in American Letters." Black World, 20, no. 2 (December, 1970), 10-11.

# VI. CRITICAL STUDIES

## 1952-1964

192. Baumbach, Jonathan. "Nightmare of a Native Son: Ellison's 'Invisible Man'." Critique, 6, no. 1 (Spring, 1963), 48-65. Reprinted in Baumbach's The Landscape of Nightmare. New York: New York University Press, 1965, pp. 68-86.

193. Bone, Robert A. The Negro Novel in America. New Haven: Yale University Press, 1958, pp. 196-212.

194. Bontemps, Arna. "Recent Writing By Negroes."
     Literature in the Modern World, William Griffin,
     ed. Lectures delivered at George Peabody Col-
     lege for Teachers, 1951-1954. Nashville, Tenn.:
     George Peabody College for Teachers, 1954, pp.
     119-122.

195. Brumm, Ursula. "The Figure of Christ in Ameri-
     can Literature." Partisan Review, 24 (1957), 403-
     413.

196. Ford, Nick Aaron. "Four Popular Negro Novelists."
     Phylon, 15, no. 1 (March, 1954), 29-39. (Elli-
     son, Motley, Wright, Yerby)

197. Fraiberg, Selma. "Two Modern Incest Heroes."
     Partisan Review, 28 (September-October, 1961),
     646-661. Reprinted in Reilly, pp. 73-79.

198. Frohock, Wilbur M. Strangers to this Ground: Cul-
     tural Diversity in Contemporary American Writing.
     Dallas, Texas: Southern Methodist University
     Press, 1961.

199. Glicksberg, Charles I. "The Symbolism of Vision."
     Southwest Review, 39 (1954), 259-265. Reprinted
     in Reilly, pp. 48-55.

200. Haslam, Gerald W. "Two Traditions in Afro-Ameri-
     can Literature." Research Studies, 37, no. 3
     (September, 1969), 183-193.

201. Hassan, Ihab. Radical Innocence: Studies in the
     Contemporary Novel. Princeton, N.J.: Prince-
     ton University Press, 1961, pp. 168-179.

202. Heermance, J. Noel. "A White Critic's Viewpoint:
     The Modern Negro Novel." Negro Digest, 13
     (May, 1964), 66-76.

203. Horowitz, Ellin. "The Rebirth of the Artist." On
     Contemporary Literature, Richard Kostelanetz,
     ed. New York: Avon Books, 1964, pp. 330-346.
     Reprinted in Reilly, pp. 80-88.

204. Horowitz, Floyd R. "Enigma of Ellison's Intellectual
     Man." CLA Journal, 7 (December, 1963), 126-
     132.

205. _____ . "Ralph Ellison's Modern Version of Brer
      Bear and Brer Rabbit in Invisible Man." Mid-
      continent American Studies Journal, 4, no. 2
      (Fall, 1963), 21-27. Reprinted in Reilly, pp. 32-
      38.

206. Howe, Irving. "Black Boys and Native Sons." Dis-
      sent, 10, no. 4 (Autumn, 1963), 353-368. Re-
      printed in Howe's World More Attractive. New
      York: Horizon Press, 1963, pp. 98-122. Re-
      printed in Five Black Authors, Donald B. Gibson,
      ed. New York: New York University Press,
      1970, pp. 254-270, and, partly, in Reilly, pp.
      100-102.

207. _____ . "A Reply to Ralph Ellison." New Leader,
      47 (February 3, 1964), 12-14. Howe's reply to
      Ellison's "The World and the Jug," which is a
      rejoinder to Howe's "Black Boys...." See "The
      Critic and the Writer--an Exchange." New Leader,
      47 (February 3, 1964), 12-22.

208. Hyman, Stanley Edgar. "The Folk Tradition." Parti-
      san Review, 25, no. 2 (Spring, 1958), 197-211.
      Reprinted in Hyman's The Promised End. New
      York: World Publishing Company, 1963. Part of
      an exchange with Ellison entitled "The Negro
      Writer in America: an Exchange," which appeared
      in the above issue of the Partisan Review.

209. Isaacs, Harold R. "Five Writers and Their African
      Ancestors." Part II. Phylon, 21, no. 2 (Winter,
      1960), 317-322.

210. Jackson, Blyden. "A Golden Mean for the Negro
      Novel." CLA Journal, 3, no. 1 (September,
      1959), 81-87.

211. Jackson, Esther M. "The American Negro and the
      Image of the Absurd." Phylon, 23, no. 4 (Winter,
      1962), 359-371. Reprinted in Reilly, pp. 64-72.

212. Klein, Marcus. "Ralph Ellison's 'Invisible Man'."
      After Alienation. Cleveland: World Publishing
      Company, 1964, pp. 71-146. Reprinted in Images
      of the Negro in American Literature, Seymour L.
      Gross and John E. Hardy, eds. Chicago:

University of Chicago Press, pp. 249-264, and in
Gottesman, pp. 74-88.

213. Knox, George. "The Negro Novelist's Sensibility and
the Outsider Theme." Western Humanities Review,
11 (Spring, 1957), 137-148.

214. Lehan, Richard. "Existentialism in Recent American
Fiction: the Demonic Quest." Texas Studies in
Literature and Languages, 1, no. 2 (Summer,
1959), 181-202.

215. Levant, Howard. "Aspiraling We Should Go." Mid-
continent American Studies Journal, 4, no. 2
(Fall, 1963), 3-20.

216. Lewis, Richard W. B. "Recent Fiction: Picaro and
Pilgrim." A Time of Harvest, Robert E. Spiller,
ed. New York: Hill and Wang, 1962, pp. 144-
153.

217. Marcus, Steven. "American Negro in Search of
Identity." Commentary, 16 (November, 1953),
456-463. Reprinted in Gottesman, pp. 2-14.

218. Maund, Alfred. "The Negro Novelist and the Contemporary Scene." The Chicago Jewish Forum,
13, no. 1 (Fall, 1954), 28-34.

219. Mebane, Mary E. "Existential Themes in Ellison's
Invisible Man and Wright's The Outsider." Lex-
ington, Ky.: The University of Kentucky Press,
1963. Kentucky Microcards, Series A, Modern
Language Series, 132.

220. Pearce, Richard. "The Walker: Modern American
Hero." Massachusetts Review, 5, no. 4 (Summer, 1964), 761-764.

221. Rovit, Earl H. "Ralph Ellison and the American
Comic Tradition." Wisconsin Studies in Contemporary Literature, 1 (1960), 34-42. Reprinted in Recent American Fiction: Some Critical Views. Joseph J. Waldmeir, ed. Boston:
Houghton Mifflin, 1963, pp. 167-174, and in
Reilly, pp. 56-63.

222. Starke, Juanita G. "Symbolism of the Negro College in Three Recent Novels." Phylon, 17, no. 4 (December, 1956), 365-373.

223. Witham, W. Tasker. The Adolescent in the American Novel 1920-1960. New York: Frederick Ungar Publishing Co., 1964, pp. 58ff.


1965-1971

224. Allen, Michael. "Some Examples of Faulknerian Rhetoric in Ellison's Invisible Man." The Black American Writer, Christopher W. E. Bigsby, ed. Vol. I: Fiction. Deland, Florida: Everett Edwards, 1969, pp. 143-151.

225. Alter, Robert. "The Apocalyptic Temper." Commentary, 41, no. 6 (June, 1966), 61-66.

226. Bell, J. D. "Ellison's Invisible Man." Explicator, 29, no. 3 (November, 1970), #19. Brief note explaining derivation of "ballin' the Jack."

227. Bennett, John Z. "The Race and the Runner: Ellison's Invisible Man." Xavier University Studies, 5, no. 1 (March, 1966), 12-26.

228. Bennett, Stephen B. and William W. Nichols. "Violence in Afro-American Fiction: An Hypothesis." Modern Fiction Studies, 17, no. 2 (Summer, 1971), 221-228.

229. Bloch, Alice. "Sight Imagery in Invisible Man." English Journal, 55, no. 8 (November, 1966), 1019-21, 1024.

230. Bone, Robert A. "Ralph Ellison and the Uses of Imagination." Tri-Quarterly, no. 6 (1966), 39-54. Reprinted in Anger and Beyond, Herbert Hill, ed. New York: Harper and Row, 1966, pp. 86-111. Reprinted in Reilly, pp. 22-31, and in Gottesman, pp. 16-37.

231. Boskin, Joseph. "The Life and Death of Sambo: Overview of an Historical Hang-up." Journal of Popular Culture, 4, no. 3 (Winter, 1971), 647-657.

232.  Boulger, James D.  "Puritan Allegory in Four Mod-
      ern Novels."  Thought, 44, no. 174 (Autumn, 1969),
      413-432.

233.  Brown, Lloyd W.  "Black Entitles:  Names as Symbols
      in Afro-American Literature."  Studies in Black
      Literature, 1, no. 1 (September, 1970), 16-44.

234.  _____.  "Ralph Ellison's Exhorters:  The Role of
      Rhetoric in Invisible Man."  CLA Journal, 13, no.
      3 (March, 1970), 289-303.

235.  Christian, Barbara.  "Ralph Ellison:  a Critical Study."
      Black Expression.  Addison Gayle, Jr., ed.  New
      York:  Weybright and Talley, Inc., 1969, pp. 353-
      365.

236.  Clarke, John Henrik.  "The Visible Dimension of In-
      visible Man."  Black World, 20, no. 2 (December,
      1970), 27-30.

237.  Clipper, Lawrence J.  "Folkloric and Mythic Elements
      in Invisible Man."  CLA Journal, 13, no. 3
      (March, 1970), 229-241.

238.  Collier, Eugenia W.  "The Nightmare Truth of an In-
      visible Man."  Black World, 20, no. 2 (Decem-
      ber, 1970), 12-19.

239.  Fass, Barbara.  "Rejection of Paternalism:  Haw-
      thorne's My Kinsman Major Molineux and Ellison's
      Invisible Man."  CLA Journal, 14, no. 3 (March,
      1971), 313-323.

240.  Fleming, Robert E.  "Contemporary Themes in John-
      son's Autobiography of an Ex-Colored Man."  Ne-
      gro American Literature Forum, 4, no. 4 (Winter,
      1970), 120-124.

241.  Fontaine, William T.  "The Negro Continuum From
      Dominant Wish To Collective Act."  African Forum,
      3, no. 4, i (Spring and Summer, 1968), 63-96.

242.  Ford, Nick Aaron.  "The Ambivalence of Ralph Elli-
      son."  Black World, 20, no. 2 (December, 1970),
      5-9.

243.  Foster, Frances.  "The Black and White Masks of
       Frantz Fanon and Ralph Ellison."  Black Academy
       Review, 1, no. 4 (Winter, 1970), 46-58.

244.  Furay, Michael.  "Négritude--a Romantic Myth."
       New Republic, 155, no. 1 (July 2, 1966), 32-35.

245.  Goede, William.  "On Lower Frequencies:  the Buried
       Men in Wright and Ellison."  Modern Fiction
       Studies, 15, no. 4 (Winter, 1969-1970),  483-501.

246.  Greenberg, Alvin.  "Choice:  Ironic Alternatives in
       the World of the Contemporary American Novel."
       American Dreams, American Nightmares.  David
       Madden, ed.  Carbondale, Ill.:  Southern Illinois
       University Press, 1970, pp. 175-187.

247.  Greene, Maxine.  "Against Invisibility."  College Eng-
       lish, 30, no. 6 (March, 1969), 430-436.

248.  Griffin, Edward M.  "Notes from a Clean, Well-
       Lighted Place:  Ralph Ellison's Invisible Man."
       Twentieth Century Literature, 15, no. 3 (October,
       1969), 129-144.

249.  Gross, Theodore L.  The Heroic Ideal in American
       Literature.  New York:  Oxford University Press,
       1971, pp. 148-179.

250.  _____.  "The Idealism of Negro Literature in
       America."  Phylon, 30, no. 1 (Spring, 1969), 5-
       10.

251.  Guttman, Allen.  "Focus on Ralph Ellison's Invisible
       Man:  American Nightmare."  American Dreams,
       American Nightmares.  David Madden, ed.  Car-
       bondale, Ill.:  Southern Illinois University Press,
       1970, pp. 188-196.

252.  Hassan, Ihab.  "The Novel of Outrage:  A Minority
       Voice in Postwar American Fiction."  American
       Scholar, 34, no. 2 (Spring, 1965), 239-253.  Re-
       printed in The American Novel Since World War
       II.  Marcus Klein, ed.  New York:  Fawcett,
       1969, pp. 196-209.

253.  Hays, Peter L.  "The Incest Theme in Invisible Man."

Western Humanities Review, 23, no. 4 (Autumn, 1969), 335-339.

254. Horowitz, Floyd R. "An Experimental Confession From a Reader of Invisible Man." CLA Journal, 13, no. 3 (March, 1970), 304-314.

255. Howard, David C. "Points in Defense of Ellison's Invisible Man." Notes on Contemporary Literature, 1, no. 1 (January, 1971), 13-14.

256. Kaiser, Ernest. "A Critical Look at Ellison's Fiction and at Social and Literary Criticism By and About the Author." Black World, 20, no. 2 (December, 1970), 53-97.

257. Kazin, Alfred. "Absurdity as Contemporary Style." Mediterranean Review, 1, no. 3 (Spring, 1971), 39-46.

258. Kent, George E. "Ethnic Impact in American Literature: Reflections on a Course." CLA Journal, 11, no. 1 (September, 1967), 24-37.

259. _____. "Ralph Ellison and Afro-American Folk and Cultural Tradition." CLA Journal, 13, no. 3 (March, 1970), 265-276.

260. Klotman, Phyllis R. "The Running Man as Metaphor in Ellison's Invisible Man." CLA Journal, 13, no. 3 (March, 1970), 277-288.

261. Kostelanetz, Richard. "The Politics of Ellison's Booker: Invisible Man as Symbolic History." Chicago Review, 19, no. 2 (1967), 5-26.

262. LeClair, Thomas. "The Blind Leading the Blind: Wright's Native Son and a Brief Reference to Ellison's Invisible Man." CLA Journal, 13, no. 3 (March, 1970), 315-320.

263. Lee, A. Robert. "Sight and Mask: Ralph Ellison's Invisible Man." Negro American Literature Forum, 4, no. 1 (March, 1970), 22-23.

264. Lee, L. L. "The Proper Self: Ralph Ellison's Invisible Man." Descant, 10 (Spring, 1966), 38-48.

265.   Lehan, Richard.   "The Strange Silence of Ralph Elli-
        son. "   California English Journal, 1, no. 2
        (Spring, 1965), 63-68.   Partly reprinted in Reilly,
        pp. 106-110.

266.   Lewis, Richard W. B.   "Days of Wrath and Laughter. "
        In his Trials of the Word:   Essays in American
        Literature and the Humanistic Tradition.   New
        Haven:   Yale University Press, 1965, pp. 184-235.

267.   Lieberman, Marcia R.   "Moral Innocents:   Ellison's
        Invisible Man and Candide. "   CLA Journal, 15, no.
        1 (September, 1971), 64-79.

268.   Lillard, Stewart.   "Ellison's Ambitious Scope in In-
        visible Man. "   English Journal, 58, no. 6 (Sep-
        tember, 1969),   833-839.

269.   Littlejohn, David.   Black on White:   A Critical Survey
        of Writing by American Negroes.   New York:   The
        Viking Press, Inc. , 1966, pp. 110-119.

270.   Ludington, Charles T. , Jr.   "Protest and Anti-Pro-
        test:   Ralph Ellison. "   Southern Humanities Re-
        view, 4, no. 1 (Winter, 1970), 31-39.   See also
        Pugh, Griffith T.

271.   Margolies, Edward.   "History as Blues:   Ralph Elli-
        son's Invisible Man. "   Native Sons:   A Critical
        Study of Twentieth-Century Negro American Authors.
        Philadelphia, Pa. :   J. B. Lippincott Co. , 1968,
        pp. 127-148.

272.   Mason, Clifford.   "Ralph Ellison and the Underground
        Man. "   Black World, 20, no. 2 (December, 1970),
        20-26.

273.   May, John R. , S. J.   "Images of Apocalypse in the
        Black Novel. "   Renascence, 23, no. 1 (Autumn,
        1970), 31-45.

274.   Mengeling, Marvin E.   "Whitman and Ellison:   Older
        Symbols in a Modern Mainstream. "   Walt Whitman
        Review, 12, no. 3 (September, 1966), 67-70.

275.   Miller, Stuart.   The Picaresque Novel.   Cleveland,
        Ohio:   Case Western Reserve University, 1967,
        pp. 134-135.

276.  Murray, Albert.  The Omni-Americans:  New Perspec-
      tives on Black Experience and American Culture.
      New York:  Outerbridge & Dienstfrey, 1970, pp.
      167, 177-178 et seq.

277.  Nash, Russell W.  "Stereotypes and Social Types in
      Ellison's Invisible Man."  Sociological Quarterly,
      6, no. 4 (Autumn, 1965), 349-360.

278.  Neal, Larry.  "Ellison's Zoot Suit."  Black World,
      20, no. 2 (December, 1970), 31-52.

279.  Nichols, William W.  "Ralph Ellison's Black Ameri-
      can Scholar."  Phylon, 31, no. 1 (Spring, 1970),
      70-75.

280.  Nower, Joyce.  "The Tradition of Negro Literature in
      the United States."  Negro American Literature
      Forum, 3, no. 1 (Spring, 1969), 5-12.

281.  O'Brien, John.  "'Becoming' Heroes in Black Fiction:
      Sex, Iconoclasm and the Immanence of Salvation."
      Studies in Black Literature, 2, no. 3 (Autumn,
      1971), 1-5.

282.  O'Daniel, Therman B.  "The Image of Man As Por-
      trayed By Ralph Ellison."  CLA Journal, 10, no.
      4 (June, 1967), 277-284.  Reprinted in Reilly,
      pp. 89-96.

283.  Olderman, Raymond M.  "Ralph Ellison's Blues and
      Invisible Man."  Wisconsin Studies in Contemporary
      Literature, 7, no. 2 (Summer, 1966), 142-159.

284.  Pearce, Richard.  "Which Way Is Up?"  Stages of
      the Clown:  Perspectives on Modern Fiction From
      Dostoyevsky to Beckett.  Carbondale, Ill.:  South-
      ern Illinois University Press, 1970, pp. 117-135.

285.  Phillips, Elizabeth C.  Ralph Ellison's Invisible Man.
      Monarch Notes.  New York:  Monarch Press, 1971.

286.  _____.  "Two Underground Men:  Richard Wright's
      'The Man Who Lived Underground' and Ralph Elli-
      son's Invisible Man."  Paper read before the Ten-
      nessee Philological Association, Memphis State Uni-
      versity, March, 1971.  Abstract in Tennessee

Philological Bulletin, 8 (July, 1971), 27-28.

287. Powell, Grosvernor E.  "Role and Identity in Ralph
     Ellison's Invisible Man."  Private Dealings: Eight
     Modern American Writers, David J. Burrows et
     al., eds.  Stockholm: Almqvist and Wiksell, 1970,
     pp. 95-105.

288. Pugh, Griffith T., Fred L. Standley, Charles T.
     Ludington, and Darwin T. Turner.  "Three Negro
     Novelists:  Protest and Anti-Protest--a Symposium."
     Southern Humanities Review, 4, no. 1 (Winter,
     1970), 17-50.

289. Radford, Frederick L.  "The Journey Towards Cas-
     tration:  Interracial Sexual Stereotypes in Ellison's
     Invisible Man."  Journal of American Studies, 4,
     no. 2 (February, 1971), 227-231.

290. Reilly, John M., comp.  Twentieth Century Interpreta-
     tions of Invisible Man.  Englewood Cliffs, N.J.:
     Prentice-Hall, 1970.

291. Rodnon, Stewart.  "The Adventures of Huckleberry
     Finn and Invisible Man:  Thematic and Structural
     Comparisons."  Negro American Literature Forum,
     4, no. 2 (July, 1970), 45-51.

292. _____.  "Ralph Ellison's Invisible Man:  Six Tenta-
     tive Approaches."  CLA Journal, 12, no. 3 (March,
     1969), 244-256.  Reprinted in Gottesman, pp. 109-
     120.

293. Rollins, Ronald G.  "Ellison's Invisible Man."  Ex-
     plicator, 30, no. 3 (November, 1971), #22.

294. Rupp, Richard H.  "Ralph Ellison: a Riotous Feast
     of the Self."  Celebration in Postwar American
     Fiction 1945-1967.  Coral Gables, Fla.: Univer-
     sity of Miami Press, 1970, pp. 151-164.

295. Sanders, Archie D.  "Odysseus in Black:  An Analysis
     of the Structure of Invisible Man."  CLA Journal,
     13, no. 3 (March, 1970), 217-228.

296. Schafer, William J.  "Irony From Underground--Sa-
     tiric Elements in Invisible Man."  Satire Newsletter,

7 (Fall, 1969), 22-28.   Reprinted in Reilly, pp. 39-47.

297. _____. "Ralph Ellison and the Birth of the Anti-Hero." Critique, 10, no. 2 (1968), 81-93. Reprinted in Gottesman, pp. 89-100.

298. Scott, Nathan A., Jr. "Judgment Marked By a Cellar: the American Negro Writer and the Dialectic of Despair." University of Denver Quarterly, 2, no. 2 (Summer, 1967), 5-35.

299. Singh, Raman K. "The Black Novel and Its Tradition." Colorado Quarterly, 20, no. 1 (Summer, 1971), 23-29.

300. Singleton, M. K. "Leadership Mirages as Antagonists in Invisible Man." Arizona Quarterly, 22, no. 2 (Summer, 1966), 157-171. Reprinted in Reilly, pp. 11-21.

301. Stanford, Raney. "The Return of the Trickster: When a Not-a-Hero Is a Hero." Journal of Popular Culture, 1, no. 3 (Winter, 1967), 228-240.

302. Tischler, Nancy. Black Masks: Negro Characters in Modern Southern Fiction. University Park, Pa.: Pennsylvania State University Press, 1969, multiple references.

303. _____. "Negro Literature and Classic Form." Contemporary Literature, 10, no. 3 (Summer, 1969), 352-365. See also Volger, Thomas A.

304. Turner, Darwin T. "Sight in Invisible Man." CLA Journal, 13, no. 3 (March, 1970), 258-264.

305. Vogler, Thomas A. "Invisible Man: Somebody's Protest Novel." The Iowa Review, 1, no. 2 (Spring, 1970), 64-82. Reprinted in Gottesman, pp. 51-74.

306. _____, and Tischler, Nancy M. "An Ellison Controversy." Contemporary Literature, 11, no. 1 (Winter, 1970), 130-135.

307. Walker, James. "What Do You Say Now, Ralph

Ellison?" <u>Black Creation</u>, 1, no. 2 (Summer, 1970), 16-18.

308. Weinberg, Helen. <u>The New Novel in America: the Kafkan Mode in Contemporary Fiction.</u> Ithaca, N.Y.: Cornell University Press, 1970, pp. 186-191 et seq.

309. Wilner, Eleanor R. "The Invisible Black Thread: Identity and Nonentity in <u>Invisible Man.</u>" <u>CLA Journal,</u> 13, no. 3 (March, 1970), 242-257.


VII.   UNPUBLISHED DISSERTATIONS


310. Britt, David Dobbs. "The Image of the White Man in the Fiction of Langston Hughes, Richard Wright, James Baldwin and Ralph Ellison." DA 29 (1968): 1532A (Emory).

311. Havemann, Carol. "The Fool as Mentor in Modern American Parables of Entrapment: Ken Kesey's <u>One Flew Over the Cuckoo's Nest,</u> Joseph Heller's <u>Catch-22</u> and Ralph Ellison's <u>Invisible Man.</u>" DAI 32 (1971): 2091A (Rice).

312. Hux, Samuel Holland. "American Myth and Existential Vision: the Indigenous Existentialism of Mailer, Bellow, Styron, and Ellison." DA 26 (1965): 5437 (Connecticut).

313. Long, Madeleine J. "Sartrean Themes in Contemporary American Literature." DA 28 (1967): 1439A (Columbia).

314. Rubin, Steven J. "Richard Wright and Ralph Ellison: Black Existential Attitudes." DAI 30 (1969): 2041A (Michigan).

315. Weinstein, Sharon R. "Comedy and Nightmare: the Fiction of John Hawkes, Kurt Vonnegut, Jr., Jerzy Kosinski, and Ralph Ellison." DAI 32 (1971): 3336A (Utah).

316. Zietlow, Edward R. "Wright to Hansberry: the Evo-
     lution of Outlook in Four Negro Writers." (Wright,
     Ellison, Baldwin, Hansberry) DA 28 (1967): 701A
     (Washington).


                          ADDENDA--U. S.


                  I.  BIOGRAPHICAL INFORMATION

317. Hunter, Marjorie. "Negro Glorifies Harlem to Sena-
     tors." New York Times, August 31, 1966. (Same
     as No. 59)

318. McCarthy, Colman. "Thinkers and Their Thoughts
     (III): Ralph Ellison and the Value of Tradition
     and Culture." The Washington Post, November
     21, 1970, p. A14.

319. Montgomery, Ed. "10 State Authors Win Library
     Week Salute." The Sunday Oklahoman, April 16,
     1967, p. 23.

# CHECKLIST: FRENCH SECONDARY MATERIAL

## 1954-1971

### I. FRENCH TRANSLATIONS--Invisible Man

1. Au delà du regard, tr. Michel Chrestien. Paris: Editions Denoël, 1954.

2. Homme invisible, pour qui chantes-tu? Tr. Robert et Magali Merle. Paris: Editions Bernard Grasset, 1969.

### II. BIOGRAPHICAL INFORMATION

3. Dommergues, Pierre. Les U.S.A. à la recherche de leur identité: rencontres avec 40 écrivains américains. Paris: Editions Bernard Grasset, 1967, p. 422.

4. Kattan, Naim. "Rencontre avec Ralph Ellison." Les Langues Modernes, 60, no. 3 (May-June, 1966), 331-333.

5. "Ralph Ellison, Chevalier des Arts et Lettres." France-Amérique, 20 March, 1969, p. 12. Brief entry and picture of award ceremony.

6. "Ralph Ellison: Notre lutte nous proclame à la fois 'Nègres' et 'Américains'," in "Enquête sur la culture noire," Preuves, no. 87 (May, 1958), 33-38. Reprinted in Shadow and Act as "Some Questions and Some Answers," pp. 253-263 (Signet paperback edition).

7. Sainville, Leonard. Anthologie de la littérature négro-africaine, II. Romanciers et conteurs. Paris: Présence Africaine, 1968, p. 615. Unresearched and partly erroneous entry.

8.  Saporta, Marc. Histoire du roman américain. Paris: Seghers, 1970, p. 328.
    Scanty; only date of birth and of I. M.'s publication given.

9.  Thinesse, Anne. "Ralph Ellison est-il autre chose qu'un Oncle Tom qui a reussi?" Le Figaro Littéraire, 11-17 August, 1969, p. 28. Interview.

10. Thompson, James, Lennox Raphael and Steve Cannon. "Ralph Ellison: la parole est à l'homme invisible." Informations et Documents, no. 250 (March 15, 1968), 22-26.
    Extracts from taped interviews conducted in New York in 1965, and originally published in the U. S. under the title "A Very Stern Discipline," Harper's Magazine, 234, no. 1402 (March, 1967), 76-95.

11. Van Tieghem, Philippe. Dictionnaire des littératures. Paris: Presses universitaires de France, 1968, I. Scanty; same dates as in Saporta.

12. Warren, Robert Penn. "Moi je suis content d'être un noir." Journal de Genève, Samedi Littéraire, No. 30, July, 1970.
    Excerpts from interview in Warren's Who Speaks For the Negro? (1965). See U. S. #64.

## III.  BIBLIOGRAPHIES

### A.  Primary

13. Dommergues, Pierre. Les U. S. A. à la recherche de leur identité: rencontres avec 40 écrivains américains. Paris: Editions Bernard Grasset, 1967, p. 422.
    Only English editions of I. M. and Shadow and Act listed. Erroneous entry regarding French translation of I. M.

14. Saporta, Marc. Histoire du roman américain. Paris: Seghers, 1970, pp. 317, 318.
    Chronology of American literary events lists short story, "Mister Toussan," for 1941 and I. M. for 1952.

## B. Secondary

15. Laude, Christiane, comp. Panorama critique du ro-
    man américain contemporain. Paris: Centre de
    Documentation Benjamin Franklin, 1967.
    Mostly English-language sources; journal articles
    are excluded.


## IV.  LITERARY HISTORIES AND HANDBOOKS

16. Brodin, Pierre. Présences contemporaines: écrivains
    américains d'aujourd'hui des années 50. Paris:
    Nouvelles Editions Demeresse, 1964.

17. Cahen, Jacques-Fernand. La littérature américaine.
    5e édition. Paris: Presses Universitaires, 1968.
    "Que Sais-Je?" series.
    No discussion of Ellison, only inclusion of him in
    a list.

18. Dommergues, Pierre. Les écrivains américains
    d'aujourd'hui. Paris: Presses Universitaires, 1965.
    "Que Sais-Je?" series.

19. _____. Les U.S.A. à la recherche de leur identité:
    rencontres avec 40 écrivains américains. Paris:
    Editions Bernard Grasset, 1967.

20. Fabre, Michel. Les Noirs américains. Paris: Ar-
    mand Colin, 1968.

21. Sainville, Leonard. Anthologie de la littérature négro-
    africaine, I. Romanciers et conteurs. Paris:
    Présence Africaine, 1963.

22. Saporta, Marc. Histoire du roman américain. Paris:
    Seghers, 1970.


## V.  REVIEWS

### 1954

23. Moussy, Marcel. "Notes de lecture: Au delà du re-
    gard." Les Letters Nouvelles, no. 16 (June, 1954),
    917-919.

1969

24. Barrière, Françoise. "Homme invisible, pour qui chantes-tu?" Lettres Françaises, 9 July, 1969, p. 4.

25. Bourniquel, Camille. "Librairie du mois: Ralph Ellison, Homme invisible, pour qui chantes-tu?" Esprit, 37 (September, 1969), 368-370.

26. Bueges, Jean. "Ralph Ellison: Homme invisible, pour qui chantes-tu?" Paris-Match, no. 1063 (20 September, 1969), p. 25.

27. Cabau, Jacques. "Nous sommes tous des nègres." L'Express, no. 936 (16-22 June, 1969), 56-57.

28. C[opperman], A[nnie]. "Homme invisible, pour qui chantes-tu?" Les Echos, 27 June, 1969, p. 16.

29. Coté, Michèle. "Entre deux mondes hostiles." La Quinzaine Littéraire, no. 78 (1-15 September, 1969), 8-9.

30. Diagne, Pathé. "Homme invisible, pour qui chantes-tu?" Présence Africaine, 74 (1970), 223-225.

31. Dommergues, Pierre. "Etude: Ralph Ellison et la Culture Noire: Un livre prophétique." Le Monde, 14 June, 1969, Literary Supplement, "Le Monde des Livres," pp. IV-V.

32. Fleury, Claude. "L'Amérique invisible." Republicain Lorrain, 7 June, 1969.

33. Freustie, Jean. "Le Noir Invisible." Nouvel Observateur, 7 July, 1969, pp. 32-33.

34. Galey, Matthieu. "Unique livre d'un Noir américain de 55 ans: un roman prophétique qui reparaît en France après 15 ans de succès aux U.S.A." Paris-Presse, 29 May, 1969, p. 2D.

35. Kyria, Pierre. "Chant de mémoire et blues de l'homme noir." Combat, 12 June, 1969, p. 7.

36. Las Vergnas, Raymond. "La Nuit Noire." Les Nouvelles Littéraires, 26 June, 1969, p. 5.

37. Lemaire, Marcel. "Homme invisible, pour qui chantes-
    tu?" Le Soir de Bruxelles, 22 October, 1969.

38. Louit, Robert. "Ralph Ellison, LeRoi Jones: De la
    révolte à la révolution." Magazine Littéraire
    (August, 1969), 35-37.

39. "Vient de paraître--Romans Etrangers: Ralph Ellison.
    --Homme invisible, pour qui chantes-tu?" Le
    Monde, 31 May, 1969, Literary Supplement, p. II.
    Publication notice.


                    VI. CRITICAL STUDIES


40. Dommergues, Pierre. "Les intellectuels dans la
    société américaine: II. La négritude." Le Monde,
    April 13, 1966, p. 3. Reprinted in Les Langues
    Modernes, 60, no. 3 (May-June, 1966), 326-330.

41. Ducornet, Guy. "Homme invisible, pour qui chantes-
    tu?" Les Langues Modernes, 63, no. 4 (July-
    August, 1969), 394-401.

42. Gérard, Albert. "Humanism and Negritude: Notes on
    the Contemporary Afro-American Novel." Diogenes
    (Montreal), no. 37 (Spring, 1962), 115-133.

43. _____. "Ralph Ellison et le dilemme noir." Revue
    Générale Belge, 97, no. 10 (October, 1961), 89-104.

44. Merle, Robert. "Preface." Homme invisible, pour
    qui chantes-tu? Tr. Robert et Magali Merle.
    Paris: Editions Bernard Grasset, 1969, pp. 7-17.

45. Petillon, Pierre-Yves. "Blues pour un mutant: Ralph
    Ellison." Critique, 24 (1968), 855-862.

46. Randall, John H., III. "Ralph Ellison: Invisible Man."
    Revue des Langues Vivantes (Brussels), 31, no. 1
    (1965), 24-44.

CHECKLIST:   GERMAN SECONDARY MATERIAL

1953-1971

I.   GERMAN TRANSLATIONS

1.   "Unruhe in Harlem." Deutsche Universitätszeitung, 10,
     no. 6 (1955), 12-13. (Translation of "Harlem Is
     Nowhere.")

2.   Unsichtbar, tr. Georg Goyert. Frankfurt/M: Fischer
     Verlag, 1954, 1969. (Translation of Invisible Man.)
     An excerpt from the Liberty Paints episode, en-
     titled "Mein erster Arbeitstag," appeared in Welt
     der Arbeit, September 24, 1954.

II.   BIOGRAPHICAL INFORMATION

3.   Brockhaus Enzyklopädie, 17th ed., Vol. V. Wiesbaden:
     F. A. Brockhaus, 1968.

4.   "Dichtervorlesung: Ralph Ellison und Paul Schallück."
     Ulmer Volkshochschule, September, 1954. (Lecture
     notice.)

5.   Ebert, Wolfgang. "Ralph Ellison in Deutschland." Die
     Zeit, September 30, 1954.

6.   Lexikon der Weltliteratur, ed. Gero von Wilpert. Stutt-
     gart: Alfred Kröner, 1963.

7.   Meyers Handbuch über die Literatur. Mannheim: Bib-
     liographisches Institut, Allgemeiner Verlag, 1964.

8.   "Ralph Ellison." Neue Presse (Frankfurt), September
     20, 1954, p. 3. (Lecture notice.)

### III.  BIBLIOGRAPHIES

#### A.  Primary

None

#### B.  Secondary

9.  Kindlers Literatur Lexikon, ed. Wolfgang von Einsie-
    del, Vol. III. Zürich: Kindler Verlag, 1964.

10. Zuther, Gerhard H. W. , comp.  Eine Bibliographie
    der Aufnahme amerikanischer Literatur in deutschen
    Zeitschriften 1945-1960.  München:  Dissertations-
    druck Franz Frankl, 1965, p. 46.

### IV.  REFERENCE WORKS AND LITERARY HISTORIES

11. Beer, Johannes, ed.  Der Romanführer, Vol. XIV.
    Stuttgart:  Anton Hiersemann, 1969.

12. Brown, John.  Panorama der modernen Literatur
    U.S.A.  Gütersloh:  Sigbert Mohn Verlag, 1964.
    (Translated from the American author's French
    original. )

13. Häusermann, Hans Walter.  Moderne amerikanische
    Literatur:  Kritische Aufzeichnungen.  München:
    Francke Verlag, 1965, p. 137.

14. Kindlers Literatur Lexikon, ed. Wolfgang von Einsiedel,
    Vol. III. Zürich: Kindler Verlag, 1964.  (Most
    useful of reference work entries. )

15. Lexikon der Weltliteratur im 20. Jahrhundert.  Frei-
    burg i/B.:  Herder Verlag, 1959/1961.  2 vols.
    (Several entries. )

16. Meyers Handbuch über die Literatur.  Mannheim:
    Allgemeiner Verlag, 1964.

17. Schönfelder, Karl Heinz and Karl Heinz Wirzberger.
    Amerikanische Literatur im Überblick.  Leipzig:
    Reclam, 1968, pp. 263-268.

18. Schulze, Martin. <u>Wege der amerikanischen Literatur:</u>
    <u>Eine geschichtliche Darstellung.</u>  Frankfurt/M.:
    Ullstein, 1968, p. 397.

19. Straumann, Heinrich.  <u>American Literature in the</u>
    <u>Twentieth Century,</u> 3rd rev. ed.  New York:  Har-
    per, 1965, p. 39.


## V.  REVIEWS

### 1953-1955

20. A. M. F.  "Amerikanische Erzähler in Übersetzungen."
    <u>Neue Zürcher Zeitung</u> (Swiss), August, 20, 1954.

21. Amf.  "Ein Neger zum Rassenproblem."  <u>National</u>
    <u>Zeitung</u> (Swiss), August 28, 1954.  (A condensed
    version of #20.)

22. [Braem, Helmut] hmb.  "Rhetoriker der Liebe."
    <u>Deutsche Rundschau</u>, 81, no. 4 (April, 1955), 419-
    420.

23. _____ M.  "Verstehen und Verzeihen:  zu zwei
    Romanen von Ralph Ellison und Alan Paton."  <u>Stutt-</u>
    <u>garter Zeitung</u>, April 10, 1954.

24. Ch.  "Ralph Ellison:  <u>Unsichtbar."  Fränkischer Volks-</u>
    <u>freund,</u> April 21, 1954.

25. Ch.  "Über das Märchen zur Wahrheit."  <u>Allgemeine</u>
    <u>Wochenzeitung der Juden in Deutschland,</u> May 29,
    1954.  (Same as #26.)

26. Ch.  "Unsichtbar."  <u>Schleswiger Holsteinische Volks-</u>
    <u>zeitung,</u> May 22, 1954.  (Same as #25.)

27. C. K.  "Unsichtbar der Roman eines Negers."  <u>Kassel-</u>
    <u>er Zeitung,</u> April 29, 1954.

28. e.  "Weil man mich nicht sehen will."  <u>Lübecker Freie</u>
    <u>Presse</u>, April 27, 1954.

29. Ehmann, Helene.  "<u>Unsichtbar."  Wiener Zeitung</u> (Aus-
    trian), October 31, 1954.

30. Eyssen, Jürgen. "Ralph Ellison: Unsichtbar." Bücherei und Bildung, 6, nos. 7/8 (July/August, 1954), 704.

31. _____. "Unsichtbar." Einkaufszentrale, Reulingen, June, 1954.

32. F. V. "Die Menschen sind unsichtbar." Der Mittag, June 10, 1954.

33. Grözinger, Wolfgang. "Kritik: Der Roman der Gegenwart." Hochland, 46 (1953-1954), 576-585.

34. H. Br. "Unsichtbar." Schweizer Bücherzeitung (Swiss), May, 1954.

35. H. L. "Ein Neger erzählt." Westfalische Nachrichten. October 25, 1954.

36. H. Th. "Ralph Ellison: Unsichtbar." Neue Tagespost, April 20, 1954.

37. HWE. "Der Unsichtbare." Hessische Nachrichten, July 10, 1954.

38. Hartl, Edwin. "Schwarze und Weisse im Roman." Die Presse (Austrian), April 25, 1954.

39. Helwig, Werner. "Dichtung im Spannungsfeld von Schwarz und Weiss." Frankfurter Allgemeine Zeitung, April 24, 1954.

40. _____. "Neger - Zivilisation - Individualismus." St. Galler Tagblatt (Swiss), May 29, 1954.

41. Hessischer Rundfunk. "Das Buch der Woche. Ralph Ellison: Unsichtbar." Radio review, April 28, 1954.

42. "'Ich bin ein Unsichtbarer ...' Amerikas 'Nationaler Buchpreis' für Ralph Ellison, einen Neger-Autor." Mannheimer Morgen, April 22, 1954.

43. "Internationaler Kulturspiegel: Die amerikanischen Bestseller 1952. ) Universitas, 8, no. 3 (March, 1953), 325-326.

44. Kaun, Axel. "Ein schwarzer Jedermann." Die Bücher-
    kommentare, no. 1 (1954), p. 3.

45. "Keiner ist der, für den ihn der andere hält." Hanno-
    versche Presse, April 3, 1954.

46. Kirn, Richard. "Roman der aüssersten Resignation."
    Frankfurter Neue Presse, March 26, 1954.

47. Koch, Thilo. "Ralph Ellison: Unsichtbar." Radio
    broadcast for program "Literarisches Wort" of
    Sender Freies Berlin, July 27, 1954.

48. Kramberg, K. H. "Abenteuer eines Unsichtbaren."
    Süddeutsche Zeitung, April 10, 1954.

49. Krämer-Badoni, R. "Zwischen den Rassen." Deutsche
    Zeitung und Wirtschafts Zeitung, June 2, 1954.

50. L. G. "Das Buch von heute: Unsichtbar." Kölnische
    Rundschau, July 14, 1954.

51. Leitenberger, Ilse. "Amerika ist aus vielen Fäden
    gewebt: über den ersten Roman des amerikanischen
    Negers Ralph Ellison." Salzburger Nachrichten
    (Austrian), May 16, 1954.

52. Lenk, Kurt. "Odyssee eines Negers." Frankfurter
    Rundschau, September 20, 1954, p. 7.

53. _____. "Zum Optimismus verdammt." Deutsche
    Studentenzeitung, June, 1954.

54. M. J. "Unsichtbar." Die Weltwoche (Swiss), May 28,
    1954.

55. ml. "Ralph Ellison: Unsichtbar." Flensburger Tag-
    blatt, August 21, 1954.

56. Neuschaefer, Friedrich. "Jenseits von Schwarz und
    Weiss." Der Tagesspiegel, May 9, 1954, p. 3.

57. Nyssen, Leo. "Die Suche nach der Wirklichkeit."
    Essener Tageblatt, June 14, 1954.

58. o. "Das Unsichtbare sichtbar zu machen." Badische
    Zeitung, June 26, 1954.

59.  P. K.  "Der Roman eines Negers."  <u>Luzerner Tagblatt</u>
     (Swiss),  July 3,  1954.

60.  Pächter, Heinz.  "Im Negerhimmel sind die Engel
     schwarz."  <u>Wort und Wahrheit</u> (Austrian),  8,  no. 1
     (January,  1953),  63-64.

61.  Piontek, Heinz.  "Ellison, Ralph:  <u>Unsichtbar.</u>"  <u>Welt
     und Wort</u>,  9 (November,  1954),  382.

62.  r. h.  "Zauber und Schrecknis."  <u>Die Gegenwart</u>,
     June 5,  1954,  pp. 375-376.

63.  "Ralph Ellison:  <u>Unsichtbar.</u>"  <u>Badisches Tageblatt,</u>
     March 23,  1954.  (Same as #64,  with addition of
     lengthy quote from Ellison. )

64.  "Ralph Ellison:  <u>Unsichtbar.</u>"  <u>Düsseldorfer Nachrichten,</u>
     April 3,  1954.  (Same as #63,  minus the quote.
     Same as #65. )

65.  "Ralph Ellison:  <u>Unsichtbar.</u>"  <u>Fränkische Presse, Bay-
     reuth,</u> April 30,  1954.  (Same as #64. )

66.  "Ralph Ellison:  <u>Unsichtbar.</u>"  <u>Oberhessische Presse,</u>
     November 30,  1954.

67.  "Ralph Ellison:  <u>Unsichtbar.</u>"  <u>Schwäbische Zeitung,</u>
     October 13,  1954.

68.  "Ralph Ellison:  <u>Unsichtbar.</u>"  <u>Solothurner Zeitung</u>
     (Swiss),  April 18,  1954.  (Same as #63. )

69.  "Ralph Ellison:  <u>Unsichtbar.</u>"  <u>Tiroler Tageszeitung</u>
     (Austrian),  April 23,  1954.

70.  "Ralph Ellison:  <u>Unsichtbar.</u>"  <u>Die Welt der Bücher</u>
     (Literarische Beihefte zur <u>Herder-Korrespondenz</u>),
     Heft 2 (1954),  105-106.

71.  Ruland, Max.  "Auf anderer Welle."  <u>Münchner Merkur,</u>
     June 16,  1954.

72.  Schallück, Paul.  "Schwarzer Odysseus."  <u>Hamburger
     Anzeiger,</u> May 8,  1954,  p. 10.  (Same as #74. )

73.  _____ .  "<u>Unsichtbar.</u>"  Dramatic adaptation of the

novel, broadcast over radio NWDR, Köln, September 23, 1954.

74. _____. "Unsichtbares wird sichtbar." Welt der Arbeit, May 14, 1954. (Same as #72.)

75. Schwab-Felisch, Hans. "Gelesen - wiedergelesen." Die Neue Zeitung, May 23, 1954.

76. "Sieger gewinnen nichts." Der Spiegel, June 23, 1954, pp. 31-32.

77. Splett, Oskar. "Ein Neger spricht für sein Volk." Schwäbische Landeszeitung, November 27, 1954.

78. Stubbe, Heinrich. "Unter der Tarnkappe." Christ und Welt, June 3, 1954.

79. Tank, K. L. "Gullivers Höllenfahrt: Neuland der amerikanischen Epik: Ralph Ellisons Roman Unsichtbar." Sonntagsblatt, May 2, 1954, p. 6.

80. "Unsichtbar (Invisible Man)." Bochumer Woche, June 27, 1954.

81. "Unsichtbar." Das Sozialblatt, September, 1954.

82. Von Zitzewitz, Monika. "Der Mensch ist unsichtbar." Die Zeit, April 1, 1954, p. 6.

83. Zacharias, Günther. "Ohne Schminke: Grossartiger Roman eines jungen Schwarzen." Die Welt, April 3, 1954.


1969-1970

84. Blöcker, Monika. "Auf Trab gehalten." Profil, 5 (Swiss, 1970), 155-158.

85. Bücherspiegel: Ralph Ellison/Unsichtbar." M. A. N. Werkzeitung-Augsburg, December, 1970.

86. C. D. "Alles Leben ist geteilt." Evangelisches Digest, June, 1970.

87. Dempf, Anneliese. "Eine verlorene Chance." Die Furche (Austrian), August 8, 1970.

88. "Der amerikanische Neger--Thema mit Variationen."
    Main Echo, November 20, 1969.

89. H. S. "Erlebnisse eines Negers." Neue Ruhr Zei-
    tung, June 1, 1970.

90. Huber, Gertrud. "Kann man Gleichheit steigern?"
    Badische Zeitung, July 6, 1970.

91. Jansen, Peter W. "Aktualität des Zorns: Schwarzer
    Roman von Ralph Ellison." Frankfurter Allge-
    meine Zeitung, April 27, 1970, p. 23.

92. Manthey, Jürgen. "Amerikanisches Abenteuer."
    Süddeutsche Zeitung, November 29, 1969.

93. "Neues auf dem Büchermarkt." Ibbenbürener Volks-
    zeitung, January 1, 1970.

94. "Neues vom Büchermarkt." Kreiszeitung für die
    Grafschaft Hoya, Syke, September 26, 1969.

95. Pilwachs, Fritz. "Ralph Ellison: Unsichtbar." Neue
    Volksbildung, 11 (Austrian, 1969), 514.

96. Reding, Josef. "Bücher für uns." Text of broadcast
    by the literature division of Süddeutscher Rundfunk,
    Stuttgart, January 29, 1970.

97. Rosenbauer, Hansjürgen. "Unsichtbar: noch einmal
    Ellison's Roman." Frankfurter Rundschau, Janu-
    ary 17, 1970.

98. "Unsichtbar." Zeitschrift für Versicherungswesen,
    December 1, 1969.

99. "Unsichtbar." Vereinigte Jugendschriften-Auschüsse
    (Arbeitsgemeinschaft GEW/BLLV Nordrhein-West-
    falen Essen).

100. "Unsichtbar im grellen Licht." Illustrierte Kronen-
     Zeitung (Austrian), July 11, 1970.

## VI. CRITICAL STUDIES

101. Brumm, Ursula. "Die Kritik des 'American Way of

Life' im amerikanischen Roman der Gegenwart. "
Jahrbuch für Amerikastudien, 9 (1964), 23-35.
(Reprinted in F. H. Link, ed. Amerika: Vision
und Wirklichkeit. Frankfurt: Athenäum Verlag,
1968, pp. 456-469. Revised version of a lecture
"Über den amerikanischen Roman der Gegenwart, "
delivered June 4, 1963 before the Deutsche Gesellschaft für Amerikastudien, and printed under the
same title in Neue Rundschau, 74 (1963), 633-646.
Cf. also, "The Figure of Christ in American Literature. " Partisan Review, 24 (1957), 403-413. )

102.         . Die religiöse Typologie im amerikanischem
        Denken. Studien zur amerikanischen Literatur und
        Geschichte, Band 2. Leiden: Brill, 1963, ch. 10.

103.  Clark, Edward.  "Images of the Negro in the Ameri-
      can Novel. " Jahrbuch für Amerikastudien, 5
      (1960), 174-184. Lecture given by the American
      author on June 29/30, 1959 to a conference of
      English teachers at Marburg.

104.  Galinsky, Hans.  "Understanding Twentieth-Century
      America Through Its Literature:  A German View. "
      Midcontinent American Studies Journal, 8, no. 2
      (Fall, 1967), 58-68.  (Several important references
      to Ellison. )

105.  Grözinger, Wolfgang.  "Der Roman der Gegenwart im
      Spiegel der Generationen. " Hochland, 46 (1953-
      1954), 576-585.

106.  Ickstadt, Heinz.  "Gesichter Babylons: zum Bild der
      Grosstadt im modernen amerikanischen Roman. "
      Jahrbuch für Amerikastudien, 16 (1971), 60-76.
      (Lecture of May 22, 1970 before the annual conven-
      tion of the Deutsche Gesellshaft für Amerikastudien
      in Berlin. )

107.  Knox, George.  "Der Totentanz in Ellison's Invisible
      Man. " Fabula, 12, nos. 2/3 (1971), 168-178.
      (Article written in English. )

108.  Nichols, Charles H.  "Color, Conscience and Cruci-
      fixion:  A Study of Racial Attitudes in American
      Literature and Criticism. " Jahrbuch für Amerika-
      studien, 6 (1961), 37-47.

109. _____ . "The Emancipation of the Negro Author."
Neusprachliche Mitteilungen, 18 (1965), 121-129.

110. _____ . "Racial Discrimination and Personal Discovery of the Ego as Reflected in Modern American Novels." Sonnenberg Briefe zur Völkever-
ständigung, 22-23 (December, 1960 - January,
1961), 6-10.

111. Orlowa, R. "Stimmen der Negerrevolution." Kunst
und Literatur, 14 (1966), 506-524.

112. Plessner, Monika. "Bildniss des Künstlers als
Volksaufwiegler." Merkur, 24, No. 267 (July,
1970), 629-643.

113. Rogge, Heinz. "Die amerikanische Negerfrage im
Lichte der Literatur von Richard Wright und Ralph
Ellison." Die Neueren Sprachen, 15 (1958), 56-
69, 103-117.

114. Rubinstein, Annette R. "Amerikanische Negerschriftsteller heute," trans. from English by Helmut
Heinrich. Sinn und Form, 20, No. 5 (September,
1968), 1264-74.

115. Wirzberger, Karl Heinz. "Probleme der Bürgerrechts-
bewegung in der amerikanischen Prosaliteratur der
Gegenwart." Sitzungsberichte der Deutschen Akad-
emie der Wissenschaften zu Berlin, Klasse für
Sprachen, Literatur und Kunst, Jahrgang 1967, No.
2, 1-36.

VII. UNPUBLISHED DISSERTATIONS

116. Feuser, Willfried. "Das Verhältnis von Individuum
und sozialer Umwelt in der Darstellung amerikanischer Negerschriftsteller 1930-1959." Frei-
burg, i. Br., 1960.

117. Müller, Hermann. "Das Problem der Toleranz in
der amerikanischen Literatur der Gegenwart."
Frankfurt/M., 1962.

176 The Blinking Eye

## APPENDIX

### GERMAN ATTITUDES TOWARD AMERICA AND HER LITERATURE

118. Ballenger, Sara Elizabeth. "The Reception of the American Novel in German Periodicals (1945-1957)." DA, 20 (1959): 1360 (Indiana). (Contains no reference to Ellison or any other Negro author.)

119. Blanke, Gustav H. "Der amerikanische Schriftsteller und die Gesellschaft: zum amerikanischen Roman des 20. Jahrhunderts." Die Neueren Sprachen, Neue Folge (1955), 153-164.

120. Blumenberg, Hans. "Mythos und Ethos Amerikas im Werk William Faulkners." Hochland, 50 (1957-58), 234-250.

121. Brumm, Ursula. "Amerika in Deutscher Sicht." Neue Deutsche Hefte, 6, nos. 63-68 (October, 1959), 636-639.

122. Bus, Heiner. "Die Figur des 'Helden' im modernen amerikanischen Roman: ein Forschungsbericht." Jahrbuch für Amerikastudien, 15 (1970), 208-220.

123. Çapek, A. "Die Pulitzer-Preise 1957 und die Situation der Literatur in den USA." Aufbau, 13 (1957), 433-437.

124. Effelberger, Hans. "Probleme der modernen amerikanischen Literatur." Die Neueren Sprachen, Neue Folge (1957), 318-324.

125. Frey, John R. "America and her Literature Reviewed by Postwar Germany." American-German Review, 20-21 (1953-55), 4-6ff.

126. _____. "Postwar German Reactions to American Literature." American-German Review, 54 (1955), 173-194.

127. Link, Franz H., ed. Amerika: Vision und Wirklichkeit. Frankfurt/M.: Athenäum Verlag, 1968.

128. _____. "Theorien zur Amerikanischen Literatur:

ein Forschungsbericht über allgemeine Darstellungen der amerikanischen Literatur. " Deutsche Vierteljahrsschrift, 36, nos. 3-4 (1962), 401-429, 582-613.

129.  Miller,  Perry.  "Das Amerikabild des amerikanischen Romans und sein Einfluss auf Europa. " Universitas, 8, no. 5 (May, 1953), 457-460.

130.  Mueller, Gustav E.  "Die amerikanische Selbstkritik im modernen Roman. " Universitas, 14 (1959), 511-520.

131.  Oppel, Horst.  "Forschungsbericht zur deutschen Amerikanistik. " Die Neueren Sprachen, Neue Folge (1959), 292-302.

132.  Ross, Werner.  "Die amerikanische Literatur als Typus. " Hochland, 55 (1962-63), 163-167.

133.  Straumann, Heinrich.  "Amerikanische Literatur in Europa:  Eine geschmackgeschichtliche Überlegung. " Anglia, 76 (1958), 208-216.

134.  Weissman, Robert.  "Tradition und Krise amerikanischer Literaturhistorie. " Weimarer Beiträge, 3 (1965), 394+.

135.  Williams, Cecil B.  "The German Picture of American Literature. " Descant, 5, no. 1 (Fall, 1960), 33-37.

# CHECKLIST: ITALIAN SECONDARY MATERIAL

## 1953-1971

### I. ITALIAN TRANSLATIONS

1. Uomo invisibile, tr. Carlo Fruttero and Luciano Gallino. Torino, Giulio Einaudi, 1956. (Translation of Invisible Man.)

2. "Volo di ritorno" in Racconti negri, ed. Carlo Izzo, tr. Lia Fromigari. Milano: Nuova Academia Editrice, 1962, pp. 183-211. (Translation of "Flying Home.")

### II. BIOGRAPHICAL INFORMATION

3. Berto, Giuseppe. "A Ralph Ellison il 'Premio Roma'." Radiocorriere, May 27-June 2, 1956. (Interview.)

4. Bulgheroni, Marisa. "Bianco e Negro." Il Mondo, February 9, 1960. ("Portrait.")

5. _____. Il nuovo romanzo americano 1945-1959. Milano: Schwarz, 1960, pp. 286, 233-241. (Includes an interview.)

6. Dizionario universale della letteratura contemporanea, III. Verona: A. Mondadori, 1960.

7. Lamberti, Luca. "Conferenza a Bari di Ralph Ellison." La Gazetta del Mezzogiorno, May 23, 1957, p. 3. (Report on a lecture at Bari.)

8. Perosa, Sergio. "Incontri con gli scrittori americani: Ralph Ellison." Corriere della sera, August 22, 1971, p. 13. (Interview.)

9. Pivano, Fernanda. America rossa e nera. Firenze: Vallecchi, 1964, pp. 240-242. (Interview.)

### III.  BIBLIOGRAPHIES

#### A.  Primary

None

#### B.  Secondary

10. Bignami, Marialuisa. "La letteratura americana in
    Italia. " Studi Americani, 10 (1964), 641-642.

11. Bulgheroni, Marisa. Il nuovo romanzo americano,
    1945-1959. Milano: Schwarz, 1960, p. 286.

12. "La letteratura afro-americana in Italia.  Nota bibli-
    ografica a cura di Stefania Piccinato. " Studi ameri-
    cani, 17 (1971), 473-505. Criticism section, 490-
    505. (Includes reviews.)

13. Repertorio bibliografico della letteratura americana in
    Italia, vols. 1-2. Roma: Edizioni di storia e let-
    teratura, 1966, p. 102. (Covers 1945-1954, and
    includes reviews.)

14. _____, vol. 3. Roma: Edizioni di storia e lettera-
    tura, 1969, pp. 133-134. (Covers 1955-1959, and
    includes reviews.)

### IV.  REVIEWS

(Note: Starred items were not available for perusal.)

15. Bertacchini, Renato. "Nuovi romanzi stranieri. "
    Gazzetta dell'Emilia, May 4, 1956.

16. Cremaschi, Inisero. "Da lustrascarpe a scrittore
    altraverso la musica jazz. " Gazzetta di Parma,
    May 1, 1956.

17. *_____. "L'uomo invisibile. " Ausonia, no. 3
    (May-June, 1956), p. 75.

18. D. "Negri d'America. " Paese-Sera, March 14-15,
    1956, p. 3.

19.   *Fontanesi, Vittorio.  "Narrativa negra."  Il Punto,
      July 7, 1956, p. 19.

20.   Fonzi, Bruno.  "Un romanzo sui negri:  L'uomo in-
      visibile."  Il Mondo, May 29, 1956, p. 6.

21.   Grana, Gianni.  "Ellison: un nuovo romanziere negro."
      La Fiera letteraria, 11, no. 27, July 1, 1956, p. 4.

22.   Lombardo, Agostino.  "The Invisible Man."  Lo Spetta-
      tore Italiano, 6 (August, 1953), 364-366.  Review
      of American edition.  Partly reprinted in Lombardo's
      Realismo e simbolismo....  See #39.

23.   Milano, Paolo.  "Le esperienze di un negro."  L'Es-
      presso, April 15, 1956, p. 12.

24.   Mirizzi, Piero.  "Un uomo invisibile."  La Gazzetta
      del Mezzogiorno, February 28, 1957.

25.   *Muzii, Enzo.  "Ricerca dell'uomo."  Il Contempo-
      raneo, June 2, 1956, p. 9.

26.   O. D. B.  "L'uomo americano in Dreiser e Ellison."
      Cinema Nuovo, April 25, 1956.

27.   P. A.  Il Paese, June 14, 1956.

28.   Padovani, Paolo.  "Notizie bibliografiche--letterature
      straniere in Italia."  L'Italia che scrive, 39, no. 8
      (August, 1956), 139.

29.   *Prisco, Michele.  "L'uomo invisibile."  Idea, June
      24, 1956, p. 4.

30.   *_____.  "L'uomo invisibile."  Leggere, 2 (May-
      June, 1956), 25.

31.   Rosati, Salvatore.  "Lettere americane: L'uomo in-
      visibile di Ralph Ellison."  Il Mondo, October 27,
      1953, p. 6.  Review of American edition.  Partly
      reprinted in Rosati's L'ombra dei padri....  See
      #40.

32.   "Uomo invisibile."  La Civiltà Cattolica, 108, i (Janu-
      ary, 1957), 90-91.

33.  *L'uomo invisibile."  Secolo XIX, May 15, 1956, p. 3.

## V.  CRITICAL STUDIES

34.  Bulgheroni, Marisa.  "Il romanzo negro."  Il nuovo
     romanzo americano, 1945, 1969.  Milano:  Schwarz,
     1960, pp. 109-130.

35.  Cambon, Glauco.  "Ralph Ellison o dell'invisibilità."
     Aut Aut (March, 1953), 135-144.

36.  Cartosio, Bruno.  "Due scrittori afroamericani:  Richard
     Wright e Ralph Ellison."  Studi Americani, 15 (1969),
     395-431.  Ellison section, 413-431.

37.  Gorlier, Claudio.  "Il figli di zio Crow.  Appunti sulla
     narrativa negra negli Stati Uniti."  Paragone Lettera-
     tura, 12, no. 140 (August, 1961), 20-32.

38.  _____.  Storia dei negri d'America.  Bologna:  Cap-
     pelli, 1963, pp. 290-294.

39.  Lombardo, Agostino.  "Il romanzo e la polemica:
     Ralph Ellison e Herbert Gold."  Realismo e sim-
     bolismo:  saggi di letteratura americana contem-
     poranea.  Biblioteca di studi americani, 3.  Roma:
     Edizioni di storia e letteratura, 1957, pp. 231-243.
     Reprint of a review in Spettatore, August, 1953,
     364-366.  See #22.

40.  Rosati, Salvatore.  "L'uomo invisibile di Ralph Ellison."
     L'ombra dei padri:  studi sulla letteratura ameri-
     cana.  Biblioteca di studi americani, 4.  Roma:
     Edizioni di storia e letteratura, 1958, pp. 135-141.
     Reprint of review in Mondo, October 27, 1953.  See
     #31.

41.  *L'uomo invisibile' in Italia."  Secolo XIX, June 11,
     1957, p. 3.

## VI.   GENERAL ESTIMATES

(Note:   References to Ellison are often
limited to a single sentence.)

42.  Bulgheroni, Marisa.  Il demone del luogo.  Milano:
     Varese, 1968, pp. 103-115.

43.  Cambon, Glauco.  "Letteratura e società in America."
     Letterature moderne, 10 (1960), 753-759.  Brief
     reference to Ellison lecture in Milan.

44.  Colombo, Furio.  "Nuova letteratura negra negli Stati
     Uniti."  Il Verri, 16 (1964), 12-41.

45.  D'Avack, Massimo.  "Solitudine negra."  La Fiera let-
     teraria, 19, April 12, 1964, p. 3.  (Discussion of
     Baldwin, unfavorably compared to Ellison.)

46.  Gorlier, Claudio.  "Letteratura americana:  cronache
     di narrativa, '61-'62."  L'Approdo letterario, 9,
     no. 21 (January-March, 1963), 145-155.  (Includes
     discussion of Baldwin, unfavorably compared to El-
     lison.)

47.  _____ .  "Letteratura nordamericana:  narrativa sotto
     inchiesta."  L'Approdo letterario, 9, nos. 23-24
     (July-December, 1963), 252-265.  (Expresses sur-
     prise at neglect of Ellison in discussions of modern
     American novelists.)

48.  _____ .  "Letteratura americana:  interrogativi sul
     Sud."  L'Approdo letterario, 14, no. 44 (October-
     December, 1968), 140-144.  (Rare reference to
     S & A in connection with discussion of Styron.)

49.  _____ .  "Letteratura americana:  la nostra America."
     L'Approdo letterario, 16, no. 49 (March, 1970), 129-
     132.  See also Portelli, Alessandro, below.

50.  Izzo, Carlo.  La letteratura nord-americana, nuova
     edizione.  Firenze: G. C. Sansoni, 1967, p. 583.
     (One sentence at the end of a 600-page book covers
     McKay, Wright, Ellison.)

51.  Lombardo, Agostino.  "Il nuovo romanzo americano."
     La ricerca del vero:  saggi sulla tradizione letter-

aria americana. Biblioteca di studi americani, 6. Roma: Edizioni di Storia e letteratura, 1961, pp. 357-369.

52. Materassi, Mario. "La facia nascosta della letteratura nordamericana." Il Ponte, 24, no. 1 (January, 1968), 62-78. (Brief mention of Ellison as among "classics" of Negro literature.)

53. _____. "Al di qua del 'Black Power': Il grido di John A. Williams." Il Ponte, 24, no. 12 (December, 1968), 1545-59. (Williams' search for the "I," leads back to Ellison's model articulation of this subject.)

54. Montalto, Dario. "Invisibilità dello zio Tom." Questioni, 4-5 (July-September, 1956), 48-52.

55. Portelli, Alessandro. "Cultura poetica Afro-Americana." Studi americani, 14 (1968), 401-429. See also Gorlier, Claudio, #49 above.


## ADDENDA--ITALY


## II. BIOGRAPHICAL INFORMATION

56. Fazio, Mario. "C'è un mondo da conquistare per i negri della vecchia Harlem." Il Secolo XIX, June 28, 1953, p. 3.

# SELECTED CHECKLIST OF BRITISH COMMONWEALTH
SECONDARY MATERIALS

## I. REVIEWS--Invisible Man

1. "Black and White." The Times, January 14, 1953, p. 9.

2. Bullough, Geoffrey. "New Novels." Birmingham Post, January 13, 1953.

3. Chaplin, Sid. "U.S. Negroes: a Great Novel." The Tribune, February 20, 1953.

4. Charques, R. D. "Fiction." The Spectator, 190 (January 23, 1953), 106.

5. Croft-Cooke, Robert. "Our Bookshelf." The Sketch, January 28, 1953.

6. Fausset, Hugh I. A. "New Novels." The Manchester Guardian, January 23, 1953.

7. Gellert, Leon. "The Refuge of Invisibility." The Sydney Morning Herald, April 11, 1953.

8. "Invisible Man." Irish Times, January 17, 1953.

9. "The Invisible Man." Book Review, broadcast over National Network, Sydney, March 29, 1953.

10. "Invisible Man." The Yorkshire Post (Leeds), January 16, 1953.

11. "Invisible Man." The Observer, May 30, 1965, p. 22. (Penguin edition. )

12. John, K. "Notes for the Novel-Reader." The Illustrated London News, March 7, 1953.

13. Laski, Marghanita. "Look-How-Nasty!" The Observer, January 11, 1953, p. 7.

14. Maclaren-Ross, J. "Private Wars." Sunday Times, January 11, 1953.

15. McKie, Ron. "Expendable!" Daily Telegraph (Sydney), Magazine Section, April 18, 1953.

16. "Narrative and Symbolism." The Scotsman (Edinburgh), January 25, 1953.

17. Price, R. G. G. "Men Against Man." Punch, January 21, 1953.

18. Rose, Jon. "Jon Rose and a Masterpiece." Books and Bookmen, 10 (September, 1965), 34. (Penguin edition.)

19. Roth, Margot. "Invisible Man." Book Review, broadcast by New Zealand Broadcasting Service, May 12, 1953.

20. "Science and Imagination." Times Literary Supplement, January 23, 1953, 53.

21. Scott, J. D. "New Novels." New Statesman and Nation, n. s. 45 (January 24, 1953), 101-102.

22. Scriblerus. "Invisibility Hides the Men of Harlem: Classic Work by New Novelist." The Chronicle (Bulawayo), March 20, 1953.

23. Spender, Stephen. "New Novels." The Listener, 49 (January 15, 1953), 115.

24. Spring, Howard. "New Books." Country Life, January 16, 1953.

25. Taggart, Joseph. "The Finger of a Saint." The Star, January 16, 1953.


II.  REVIEWS--Shadow and Act

26. "An American, a Negro." Times Literary Supplement, January 18, 1968, pp. 49-50.

27. Brogan, Daniel W. "Wholly American." The Listener, 77 (February 16, 1967), 236.

28. Crawley, Phillip. Newcastle Journal, December 24, 1966.

29. Deakin, N. D. "Shadow and Act." Race, 9 (October, 1967).

30. Jacobson, Dan. "Ellison's Essays." New Statesman and Nation, 73 (January 20, 1967), 82.

31. Larkin, Philip. "Gulliver's Travails." Manchester Guardian, January 13, 1967.

32. Melly, George. "How to Beat 'That Boy.'" The Observer, February 5, 1967, p. 26.

33. Nye, Robert. "Words That Will Bleed." The Scotsman, January 7, 1967.

34. "Shadow and Act." Northern Echo, March 31, 1967.

35. "Shadow and Act." Sunday Times, February 5, 1967.

36. Snowman, Daniel. The Tribune, February 3, 1967.

37. Tanner, Tony. "Invisible Man." The Spectator, 218, no. 7228 (January 13, 1967), 47.

38. Turner, Julian. "Shadow and Act." The Queen, January 4, 1967.


III.   CRITICAL STUDIES

39. Allen, Walter. The Modern Novel in Britain and the United States. New York: Dutton, 1964, pp. 217-219, 321-322.

40. Lowry, Malcolm. "To Albert Erskine," May, 1952. Selected Letters of Malcolm Lowry, Harvey Breit and Margerie Bonner Lowry, eds. Philadelphia: J. B. Lippincott Co., 1965, pp. 315-318.

41. McCormick, John. Catastrophe and Imagination: an Interpretation of the Recent English and American

Novel.   London:   Longmans  Green  &  Co. ,  1957.
Numerous  references.

42.   Millgate,  Michael.   American Social Fiction:   James to
      Cozzens.   London:   Oliver and Boyd,  1964,  p.  204.

43.   Rao,  B.  R.   "The Invisible Man:   a Study."   In Maini,
      Darshan Singh,  ed.   Variations on American Litera-
      ture.   New Delhi:   U. S.  Education Foundation in
      India,  1968,  pp.  93-98.

44.   Tanner,  Tony.   "The Music of Invisibility."   The City
      of Words:   American Fiction 1950-1970.   New York:
      Harper and Row,  1970,  pp.  50-63.

45.   Waghmare,  J.  M.   "Invisibility of the American Negro:
      Ralph Ellison's Invisible Man."   Quest (Bombay),  59
      (1968),  23-30.

# AUTHOR-EDITOR INDEX TO CHECKLISTS

(Numbering refers to checklist numbers)

A. M. F. (Ger. ), 20
Amf. (Ger. ), 21
Abrahams, Roger D. (U. S. ), 134
Allen, Michael (U. S. ), 224
Allen, Walter (Brit. ), 39
Alter, Robert (U. S. ), 225
Anon. (Brit. )
  Reviews, Invisible Man, 1, 8-11, 16, 20
  Reviews, Shadow and Act, 26, 34-35
Anon. (Ger. )
  Biographical, 8
  Reviews, Unsichtbar, 42, 43, 45, 63-70, 76, 80, 81, 85,
    88, 93, 94, 98-100
Anon. (It. )
  Reviews, Uomo Invisibile, 32, 33, 41
Anon. (U. S. )
  Biographical, 1, 2, 8-12, 16, 19, 20, 22-24, 26-29, 32-
    38, 45, 46, 48, 49, 51, 54-59, 62, 65, 66
  General Estimates, 173, 175, 176, 189
  Reviews, Invisible Man, 97, 98, 111, 128
  Reviews, Shadow and Act, 135, 143, 153
Arts et Lettres, Ordre des (Fr. ), 5
Au delà du regard (Fr. ), 1


Baily, Lugene (U. S. ), 70, 81
Balakian, Nona (U. S. ), 158
Ballenger, Sara Elizabeth (Ger. ), 118
Barbour, Floyd B. (U. S. ), 184
Barrett, William (U. S. ), 94
Barrière, Françoise (Fr. ), 24
Baumbach, Jonathan (U. S. ), 192
Beer, Johannes (Ger. ), 11
Bell, J. D. (U. S. ), 226

Hoffman, Frederick J. (U.S.), 164
Homme invisible, pour qui chantes-tu? (Fr.), 2
Horowitz, Ellin (U.S.), 203
Horowitz, Floyd R. (U.S.), 204, 205, 254
Howard, David C. (U.S.), 255
Howard, Vilma (U.S.), 5
Howe, Irving (U.S.), 109, 206, 207
Huber, Gertrud (Ger.), 90
Hughes, Carl Milton [Pseud.] (U.S.), 165
Hughes, Langston (U.S.), 110
Hunter, Marjorie (U.S.), 59, 317
Hux, Samuel Holland (U.S.), 312
Hyman, Stanley Edgar (U.S.), 142, 208


Ickstadt, Heinz (Ger.), 106
Igi, Eka (U.S.), 183
International Library of Negro Life and History (U.S.), 47
Isaacs, Harold R. (U.S.), 209
Izzo, Carlo (It.), 2, 50


Jackson, Blyden (U.S.), 210
Jackson, Esther M. (U.S.), 211
Jackson, Miles M. (U.S.), 144
Jacobson, Dan (Brit.), 30
Janeway, Elizabeth (U.S.), 145
Janowitz, Morris (U.S.), 146
Jansen, Peter W. (Ger.), 91
Jeffers, Lance (U.S.), 184
John, K. (Brit.), 12
Johnson, Alicia L. (U.S.), 185


Kaiser, Ernest (U.S.), 186, 256
Kattan, Naim (Fr.), 4
Kaun, Axel (Ger.), 44
Kazin, Alfred (U.S.), 112, 166, 257
Kent, George E. (U.S.), 258, 259
Killens, John O. (U.S.), 113
Kindlers Literatur Lexikon (Ger.), 9, 14
Kirn, Richard (Ger.), 46
Klein, Marcus (U.S.), 172, 212, 252
Klotman, Phyllis R. (U.S.), 260
Knox, George (Ger.), 107
Knox, George (U.S.), 213
Koch, Thilo (Ger.), 47

## GENERAL INDEX
(References are to page numbers)

Juneteenth, " 9
"The Roof, the Steeple, and the People, " 9
Nonfiction
"The Art of Fiction: An Interview, " 90n. 6
"Brave Words For a Startling Occasion, " 91
"Harlem Is Nowhere, " 101
"Tell It Like It Is, Baby, " 120
"That Same Pain, That Same Pleasure, " 24
"The World and the Jug, " 17
Emanuel, James A. , 9, 29
Emerson, Ralph Waldo, 47, 58, 78, 82n. 16, 100, 106n. 24
Eyssen, Jürgen, 94

Fabre, Michel, 9, 69
Fanon, Frantz, 41-42, 49
Fass, Barbara, 47
Faulkner, William, 47, 79n. 3, 86, 92, 96, 103n. 4
Fiedler, Leslie, 21, 36, 59n. 1
Fifteen Modern American Authors, 28
Le Figaro Littéraire, 73
Fischer Verlag, S. , 85, 89, 98
Five Black Writers, 10, 29, 30
Fleming, Robert E. , 49
Fontaine, William T. , 57
Fonzi, Bruno, 117
Ford, Nick Aaron, 34, 36, 46
Foster, Frances, 42, 49
Fraiberg, Selma, 34
Frankfurter Allgemeine Zeitung, 89, 89n. 5, 96, 104n. 5
Freedom, 15
Freud, Sigmund, 32
Frey, John R. , 86, 103n. 2
Frohock, Wilbur M. , 35
Fuller, Hoyt W. , 19
Furay, Michael, 57

Gaines, Ernest, 49
Galey, Matthieu, 73
The Garies and their Friends, 49
Gerard, Albert, 76
Germany, Anonymous reviews, Unsichtbar, 92, 97-98, 106n. 21
Initialled reviews, Unsichtbar,
Ch. , 91n. 8, 95, 104n. 8
F. V. , 93-94n. 14, 105n. 14
r. h. , 89n. 5, 103-104n. 5

General Index

213

Steinbeck, John, 79n. 3
Storia dei negri degli Stati Uniti, 119
Storia della letteratura americana, 121-122n. 6
Strangers to This Ground, 35
Straumann, Heinrich, 88
Studi Americani, 112, 114-115, 119, 121n. 3
Studies in Invisible Man, 11, 30
Styron, William, 43, 101
The System of Dante's Hell, 56

Tank, K. L., 93, 104-105n. 13
Their Eyes Were Watching God, 49
Thinesse, Anne, 67, 73, 80n. 6
Thoreau, Henry David, 35, 78, 82n. 16
A Time of Harvest, 21
Tischler, Nancy, 9, 43, 44, 56
Too Late the Phalarope, 95
Toomer, Jean, 28
Toppin, Edgar, 7
Thorp, Willard, 22
Transatlantic Migration: the Contemporary American Novel
    in France, 79n. 3
The Trials of the Word, 40, 45
Turner, Darwin T., 9, 24, 38
Twelve Great American Novels, 29
Twentieth Century Interpretations of 'Invisible Man': a Col-
    lection of Critical Essays, 7, 10, 30, 51

Ulysses, 4, 42, 43
Uncle Tom's Cabin, 99
University of Nevada, Modern Authors Library, 9
Les USA à la recherche de leur identité: rencontres avec
    40 écrivains américains, 70-71, 73, 76-77, 81n. 14

Van Tieghem, Philippe, 68
Van Vechten, Carl, 22
Velde, Paul, 18
Vogler, Thomas A., 44, 51
Von Zitzewitz, Monika, 93

Waiting For the End, 59n. 1
Walker, James, 26, 38
Warren, Robert Penn, 17, 54, 67
Washington, Booker T., 39